Eternal Heartland:

Highway 80

John T. Eber, Sr.

MANAGING EDITOR

A publication of

Eber & Wein Publishing

Pennsylvania

Foreword

As we are now into April and have just released the first volume of *Eternal Heartland*, a wonderfully talented Southern poet comes to mind. Robert Penn Warren, born on April 23, 1905, graced America with his multifaceted talent until his death in 1989. A Kentucky native, Warren's early work appeals to the old, southern traditional school of poetry practiced by the famous Fugitives in the early 1920s. Alongside fellow Fugitives John Crowe Ransom and Allen Tate, Warren contributed poems that were strictly formal in style, form, technique, and language, as his colleagues and mentors adhered to a firm belief that poetry must always be severely distinguishable from prose. Warren, however, had a free-spiritedness about him that eventually defied the poetic customs of the established group, and so he made a graceful transition from formal verse to a freer, less rigid form of poetry. Soon after, an even newer direction towards fiction brought him a Pulitzer Prize not only for his novel, *All the King's Men*, but later for his poetry as well. The only writer in America to ever receive a Pulitzer in both genres, Warren never relied on one particular style of writing to express himself and the ideas that flooded his head.

I mention Warren because I think his work is a wonderful educational tool for aspiring writers. The verse of many renown poets has their official stamp of style on it, like their own personal namebrand of poetry. However, this is what makes Warren's poetry so unique—he doesn't have a style. He wrote whatever he wanted, however he wanted, ceaselessly engaging in many styles and techniques. I find the variation found throughout his work indeed fascinating and ingenious. So the next time you find yourself in the proverbial rut or simply want to try something new, pick up a collection of Warren's poetry and allow yourself to be inspired. A true product of the South, Warren sought to express his ideas concerning America's heartland in every way possible, never placing limits or restraints on the imagination.

John Eber Sr.

She Is . . .

She is precious, pink things wrapped with a b...
She is beauty, innocence, and intelligence in t...
She is butterfly kisses with love and surprises in ...
She is smiles and giggles to sprinkle and ador...
She is petal blossoms with morning dew
She is all things perfect and a little princess too
She is an angelic saint from heavens above
She is a symbol of purity like the brightest, whitest d...
She is a fairy with sparkles of happiness galore
She is a shooting star headed for the planets, sun, and so mu...
She is a magical mermaid swimming deep into the blues
She is everything and more as prayed for on bending kr...
She is sweetness with a touch of spice since the day she wa...
She is bundle of love with a bond that can never be tor...
She is charming and irresistible with every carefree whir...
She is loving and warm like the most elegant blanket
right down to the trim
She is more valuable than the priceless, gorgeous pearl
She is the one and only, our special little girl.

Melody Anne Pressley
Oak Island, NC

A Hot Croc

Large,
medium,
or small,
any size,
a hot croc
lying in the
hot sun.
Large,
medium,
or small,
any size,
it matters, a
hot croc lying
in the hot sun.
Moving tail,
snapping jaws,
wide eyes,
very hungry.
It is a hot,
hungry croc.

Morgan Williams
Encino, CA

My Soldier's Hands

These hands protect me over the ocean in a war-torn city
These hands comforted me as I was able to sleep at night
These hands assured me that my freedom was secure
These hands touched my most prized possession
As I let my angel go—
These hands loved her like no one else could

These hands protected her as only he knows how
These hands caressed her as their child was conceived
These hands will carry that newborn babe
These hands will guide this child through life
These hands will teach that child all that's in him

These hands are tired now as I grow old
And when my time is near—
These hands will pray until my Savior appears

Nona Reedinger
Tower City, PA

I wrote this poem and said "My Soldier's Hands" because this young soldier has changed my life and became a part of my soul. It also includes two others that mean the world to me. They are Lieutenant Corporal Garrett C. Rice, U.S. Marine Corps, my granddaughter, Amber Hoover Rice, and my first great-grandchild, Connor James Rice. To all soldiers everywhere, thank you.

Silence

Silence is nothing and it's everything
It's my place, my peace, my refuge
Silence is my strength, my weakness
My treasure, my day and night

Listen to the silence, listen . . .
Nothing else than the deep breathing of a soul
It's a soul convicted to suffering
The reason's beyond a painful wound

Listen . . .
Listen to the brave spirit of solitude
To the whispering of leaves with attitude
To the still state of mind some thoughts pronounce
To the resigned silence, the body announce

Nothing in the surroundings
Nothing on the mind
Just a hand wanting to hold you
A gay memory deep inside a heart

With the silent sound of a glance upon the sky
Laconic words try to penetrate a life
They call upon your presence on my present
They crave your ardent fire

Maria A. Rivera
Miami, FL

Memories

All the time of every day
Every experience and event,
How our lives have been spent,
Those events won't last forever.
As our lives pass, life itself changes in every way,
But we don't live in those moments,
The moments live in us.
We share these moments with others.
Though we may go our separate ways,
Memories will always keep us together.

Dylan S. Lawson
Ft. Pierce, FL

I Belong

We went out in the backyard
behind a bush.
We took down our pants
and I saw him and he saw me.
Mom called out, "Lunch is ready,"
and "What are you doing?"
We said, "We're playing hide and seek,"
but really we were sneaking a peak.
We went to lunch.
I felt like I belonged to the bunch.
Cool!

Helen M. Cichy
Round Lake, IL

Devastated

To overwhelm,
To destroy,
To be left alone,
That is me.
I picture myself making in this dark forest
With the sounds of the animals of the night roaming free.
I am walking with the rustling of leaves crunching under my feet.
Buried alive in a shallow grave, my eyes wide open, gasping for air;
Who put me there?
I know I am not alone.
My eyes filled with tears,
Tears of fear.
I will not let self-pity control me.
You learn from your mistakes as others do.
Promising never to do them again is a lie too.
When silver is not good enough, the brown will make you cheap,
At this point and time, all I could do was weep.
Crying will get you nowhere
When life is not fair.
Passing out all that green
Made me evil and mean.
I am still alone,
But not as devastated.
I did learn from my mistakes and I hope you will, too.

Juanita Wright
Worcester, MA

Always Your Friends

Sometimes it's hard to write the words
That you, my dear, should see,
Or say the things that you need to hear
Or be as I should be.

You grow so fast and learn so much,
It's hard for me each day
To say or do just what is best
To help along the way!

Should I be silent or give advice?
Should I answer yes or no?
Should I control, set many rules
Or simply let you go?

One thing is certain; I'll make mistakes,
And some will seem hard to mend,
But nothing else seems clear right now
Know that you can always count on me as your friend
You mean so much to me.

Carlena M. Greenup
Georgetown, KY

The Storm

The branches obedient to the voice of the wind
Swag back and forth
And the tree shakes as gentle tears
Wash over him
The Earth's mouth opens wide
Drinking until she is full
Now storm clouds like a warring army
March through the heavens
Crushing the tiny clouds
They etch out their countenance
The rain heavy beats upon the ground
Under its weight her heart sinks deep
Lighting lifts his sword
As his steed moves fast
And fire dances across the sky
Searching where to strike
Fear rattles the tree
He bends low and waits
Until the storm is over.

Jo Worthington
Lakeland, FL

You Thought Me into Your Life

You made me in the center of Your every thought
Toward me, are good for me and not evil.
From the height of the highest sky
To the floor of the deepest sea,
I don't have to have time from You to steal,
And I don't have to ask the question why,
For You know my every action,
And You know my every reaction.
My thoughts are overwhelmed
By the care You give me, by Your outstretched arms.
I never have the need to fear alarm,
You care for me in every season under the sun.
You lead me and guide me
By Your light shining through me.
You wrote me into life with Your every thought.
You formed every part of me.
Like a book, You have opened me,
And have read every word you have formed in me
In the corner of Your thoughts toward me.
From Heaven up above,
You thought me into life by Your abounding love.

Clifford J. Seab
Chattanooga, TN

Other Mothers

Memories become so precious when Mother's Day draws near,
But there are other mothers who never get any cheer.

They bottle-fed the babies and changed their diapers too,
And later on they dressed them and sent them off to school.

They fried your favorite apple pies and baked your favorite dish,
And when you came back from the lake, they even cleaned your fish.

Who is this other mother who never gets any attention
And whose name is never mentioned?

It is none other than our mothers-in-law that we are talking about,
So let's stand up and praise them and give them a shout.

Berta D. Cook
Graham, NC

At seventy-five years old, I am visually impaired. It was a blessing to start writing poetry. Since then, I have written many poems, but this particular poem speaks for itself. Many poems and songs have been written about mothers, but often mothers-in-law are the brunt of jokes and not appreciated. Hopefully this poem will cause readers to realize what a blessing a mother-in-law can be.

A Painting in the Dark

Stars are truly beautiful
on a dark and cloudless night,
from the first one to appear above
until the last fades out of sight.

So many of them fill the sky,
these dots to human eyes.
They twinkle, shine and sparkle
after the night gives rise.

Stars decorate the depth of space
when nighttime does embark.
A masterpiece comes to the fore,
a painting in the dark.

Always present, yet well hidden
behind the light of day.
Only when the sunlight passes
comes the glorious display.

Though humans cannot fathom
the billions beyond sight,
we all can still appreciate
a lovely star-filled night.

Denise C. Hayden
Preston, CT

Broken Love

I yearn for "us."
Two helpmeets
With one soul,
One purpose, one mind,
The souls that loved each other
And had the purpose of growing together
Spiritually, emotionally, and physically.
The minds that supported, encouraged, and blessed each other.
And then you gave me a broken love,
A love that ripped my soul in pieces,
Destroyed our purpose,
And betrayed my mind.
A broken love that hurts,
Penetrates, and upsets
The heart, the chest, the stomach.
It makes a mockery of sweet memories,
And love words spoken.
A broken love is powerful,
And I refuse
To let it break me.

Bridgette C. Williams
Norfolk, VA

Crosses

In Normandy, if you go
You'll see crosses row on row
Those were people, this we know
Long forgotten until now

They were human like we are
But their life did not go far
Given up for stripe and star
In a land from home afar

Anniversaries give us thought
Those were men who here fought
But they died when live they ought
And thus our freedom they bought

But do we them now honor
All the things they fought for
No, we still wage unjust war
And plant crosses as before

Charles J. Fickey
Silver Spring, MD

You Didn't

I put up a wall
Hoping you'd climb it
When you didn't
I felt betrayed
I put up a front
Hoping you'd see through it
When you didn't
I was disappointed
I'll take my life and
Hope you'll realize
How much you mean to me
When you don't
Only then will I realize
It's all an infatuation

Erin M. Bifferato
Elkton, MD

If She Only Knew . . .

If she only knew what you told me last night
While kissing my forehead
And holding me tight.
I woke up to you
Halfway through the night,
As you looked at me and said,
"I want to make things right."
You kissed my lips and softly said,
"I'll love you forever."
And we went back to bed.
I woke up the next morning
To you on the phone,
And I heard you saying,
"She doesn't leave me alone."
From right then and there,
I decided I'm through,
Because there's no point for me
To keep running back to you.
I ran into my room
And then slammed my door
As I instantly felt my heart tear once more,
And then I felt myself slam onto the floor.

Erin A. Koch
Schnecksville, PA

Eclipsed

Pacing . . .
counting the long strides
on weather-beaten walkways
that succumb to mood swings.
Rumors left by strangers
can leave a city looking worn.
The whisper-thin outlines
of full moon disappears
and everything is cast in black and white.
The night remains totally unguarded
by the colors of regimen.
In an uncertain world,
the shadows can hide many things.
At times, we feel worlds apart,
but simple things do the trick.
Perhaps my pacing
and deep thoughts for success
have softly touched
the minute seconds of our lives
that quiet the baroque bravado
of this bold city
so we can truly appreciate
a moonless night.

Yvonne A. Gannon
Kaneohe, HI

Light or the lack of light makes the nights a fascinating study. On nights of a lunar eclipse, I feel transformed into a playful shadow blending in with the dark colors, darting in and out of festivities amongst friends, flickering the city lights. A lunar eclipse is but a mediocre phase and a chance happening, and I remain steadfast in my belief that every night is to be enjoyed. My spirits remain upbeat knowing that the moon will once again be full.

The Falls: The Bridge of Beauty

There is a place where peace can grow
In the middle of our lives; now is the time, I know.

But when we cannot get there as far as we can see,
Our mind shall hold the picture, forever it will be.

Listen to its beauty, how nature did intend.
Undisturbed by others, the beauty of the bend.

The water rushes slowly, and if you close your eyes,
The sound will bring you quickly a glimpse you can't deny.

And if you're very lucky to share it with a friend,
The peace and its beauty shall live and then extend.

The souls of our nature, it lives with our hearts,
It forever runs on beauty, and sparkles when we part.

Cindy Miller
New Carlisle, IN

My Prayer

Bless us, heavenly Father,
Forgive our erring ways.
Grant us strength to serve You
Put purpose in our days.
Give us understanding,
Enough to make us kind
So we may love all people
With our hearts and not our minds.
Teach us to be patient
In everything we do,
Content to trust Your wisdom
And to follow after You.
Help us when we pray.
Receive us in Your kingdom
To dwell with thee one day.

Dolores V. Lyons
Erie, PA

So Close, So Far

He is my man
I love him so much
He is only for me
So far, so close apart
No one else can compete
So close, so far apart
Down poured the rain really fast
Please don't tell me our love won't last
So close, so far apart
He holds the only key to my heart
Nothing could ever break us apart
This must be a huge mistake
There could never be another (looks like me)
Beautiful with eyes that look like mine
People always telling lies
So close, so far apart
Life is so unpredictable
Never knew how close to home this could really be
I received a phone call saying Daddy tried to touch me
So far, so close apart
I feel really weak
Almost immobile, can't speak
Feels like a big Mack truck
Ran me over
I cry, cry, cry
Asking myself why

Rita J. Harris
Pittsburgh, PA

Just with a Smile

In a blink of an eye
It changes from a moan
To a sigh

In a drop of a rain
It changes from plaid
To plain

In a loose hold
It changes from warm
To cold

In a strike of a drum
It changes from plush
To plum

In a beat of a heart
It changes from dull
To bright

In a strum of a guitar
It changes from ice
To water

And in a tick of a second
It changes from an impression
To an expression—
Just with a smile

Esther A. Appiah
Westerville, OH

Who Am I?

I pause a moment to reflect on years gone by.
What I have done or failed to do?
What has happened to my hope of yesterday?
Health slows my life to the simplicity of a child.
My dreams are thoughts of what could have been.
I painted the sun, rising and setting.
I danced with the wind and sang with the birds.
I rode to the hilltop, sat, and reflected.
I was a tower of strength and lover of life.
But now, I only dream and remember.
Don't wait! Do now what should be done.
Treasure each moment as it may never come again.
Hold close those who are dear,
So tomorrow there will be no regrets.
Be as you wish to be remembered.
May I be remembered for my love of others,
My compassion, strength, and dreams for tomorrow!
I am important! Each person I have helped
Has changed the outcome of future years.
May I bring a smile to all those who remember me.

Carol A. Chiaradonna
Lynn, MA

I was always shy, kept to myself. I loved to sing, read, write, sew, horseback ride, dance, and fish. Family was always my strength and inspiration. We laughed through good times and helped console each other through bad. My mother and sister inspired me in my younger years. My husband and daughters inspired me as years went by. A stroke made life very difficult for me. My family helped me refocus my life and move on. We find our needs are few, our blessings many; we have each other. I've learned to hold on to what is important, family and faith.

21

The Quantum Light

The information is there to share
from the work and inspiration of the scientific generation.

In light, a vital part of everyday life but very, very low below,
is found the photon, part of the basic foundation of creation,
a wave or a particle but not a wavy particle, we know.

In a state of excitement with the power of the sun,
along with the electron in an atom, it gets its work done.

With certainty uncertain, they have breached the curtain.
Is this a flash of light or a spark of life?
Not a physicist or mathematician am I,
but to understand the quantum jump, I try.

Holograms, light emitting diodes, laser beams
and scanning tunneling microscopes
now are products of great men's dreams.

With the macrocosm as above and the microcosm so below
in the quantum universe, what direction shall we go?

Is this all or will the scientific future determine
the Earth's rise or fall?

Bernard A. Simon
Pacifica, CA

Divorce

This "plan" is such a hard
Thing to decipher.
We're always thinking this marriage
Would be a lifer.

Not understanding why we change,
Altering our children's lives,
And we, as a couple, having to rearrange.
No child should be used as a ping-pong ball,
Bouncing back and forth.

The love of both parents,
Whether together or apart,
Should only grant their children
The love from their hearts.

Staying unhappily together for many years
Only brings out the bitterness and a lot of tears.

Oleta P. Braley
Rochester, NY

Reflections

While walking on the beach
  and deep in thought,
I think of the things
  that can't be bought.
The flow and ebb
  of the waves on the shore,
the grace of the seagulls
  on high as they soar.
The marshmallow clouds
  in a sky of blue,
ever-changing their pattern
  as they pass in review.
The sand and the rocks
  reflecting ever so bright,
as each wave rushes in
  in the dawn's early light.
No artist can duplicate
  the picture I see.
It's a painting from Heaven,
  and all of it's free.

Janice G. Harney
Plymouth, MA

The Sculpture's Crown

A grain of sand drifted ashore.
Contained within it was the world before.

It reflected the sunshine and mellowed the blue
Of watery ages only it knew.

It pondered the plight where it began,
How it arrived at being exposed to Man.

Aimlessly, it tossed, to no avail,
A pioneer of faith blazing a trail.

As it accepted its fate, a child grew aware
Of its presence and virtue, none could compare.

So she gathered its neighbors, and to its delight,
She sculpted a castle throughout the night.

Until the tide rushed in and kissed the shore,
That grain of sand was king forevermore.

Barbara J. Westbie
Magalia, CA

Sometimes in simple settings, nuggets of the infinite are captured by accident. The refined essences give each of us an unobstructed point of view that otherwise we would overlook. This intimate visual of the grains of sand was inspired many years ago by my children's carefree play along a beach near San Diego, California, as they splashed in the Pacific, and for the most part, sat serenely by the water, totally absorbed in their dream realities. It occurred to me how intricate and necessary are all the small steps in life it takes to capture our dreams.

Our Mothers

Remembering our mothers is a joy
How hard they all do toil
Day after day
From sunup to sundown
Budgeting and making things do
Trying to equal everything out in the end
Starting as a new bride
Adjusting to new surroundings and a new husband
Household chores are never ending
Many times, outside the home, a job
Remembering how many things my grandmother did without
Modern conveniences are such a big help
In time, along come little ones, sons and daughters
Growing up years will bring many fond memories
Mothers sacrificing so the little ones have what they need
Especially for many special occasions
Mother is growing older as we, the children, mature
Right before our eyes, we have seemed not to notice
Not long and she will be a grandmother
To our children, another generation
With so much love in her heart
She continues to nurture
My mother, our mothers
Praying you will never have to depart from us too soon

Caroline Caulum
Onalaska, WI

The Dogwood

Dogwood tree, will you
see your first winter through?
Last fall, I planted you with care,
savoring the buds you'd bear
when April comes.

But look at you now,
half-buried in snow,
so puny and small.
Will you grow strong and tall
when April comes?

Will the beauty that slumbers
in your limbs now so bare
awaken to blossom
pink-lipped and fair
when April comes?

As the snows come, then go
when March winds disappear,
the dogwood and I
will have spring's promise to share
when April comes.

Bill Abramson
Trenton, NJ

I attend a Mercer County Community College in New Jersey creative writing class, among others, where I maintain a 4.0 GPA. I am an animal lover and enjoy being with people. I relate to an era unfamiliar to many persons, and my poetry is reflected by personal experience. I am ninety years of age, and like the Energizer bunny, I hope to keep going and going and going.

Man-Made Pain

Rivers of red attempt to
wash away the sins of the black land
and the hardened creatures who lie within.
Souls stray from their path as the master
draws the razor harder against the wrists
of the innocent in a mistakable thought
that the flowing of sin is better than knowing
it is all your fault.
And no one cries as the master dies
and the soul flies up, only to be
rejected by Heaven so it floats to Hell
only to writhe and burn. Stuck on
limbo longing for life to fix what pain
it didn't cause. Crying for help like in life,
afraid that like sin, pain is inescapable,
so they continue to run until death,
and after death catches them and throws
them into the unknown, which seems to
ease their pain and yet, they must live
with the memory that no one cried,
no one cared, and all they did to try
and change the land of sin was in
vain, just like their death that didn't help.
Even now, they never escape their man-made pain.

Ami D. Letellier
Bennington, NH

Let Freedom Ring

Let freedom ring loud and clear
from sea to sea.
Ring loud on lands not free,
for men who died to keep me free,
for soldiers young and old to hear them in every ring.
Wave the great red, white, and blue,
red for bloodshed,
white for souls,
blue for Heaven above.
For the love of their country, they gave their lives.
Never to be forgotten,
they shine in the midnight skies.
Thank you, soldiers, one and all,
in every wave of our flag.
Although loved ones have gone,
memories of them will never be forgotten.
Let freedom ring.

Patricia M. Bilodeau
Merrimac, MA

Haiti Destruction

Sad faces all around
Destruction all over town
Doctors and nurses working overtime
With a smile and also a frown.

People sleeping in the streets
Looking around for food to eat
Sleepless night with nowhere to go
Not even a grocery store.

Tempers flaring thinking there is no hope
Trying to see how they will cope
Women and children found alive
From beneath the rubble, there is a reason why.

Don't give up, just remain strong
Help is on the way, and it won't be long
Streets and buildings are crumbling down
Destruction can and will be found.

Families are searching for one another
Mom, dads, sisters, and brothers
Keep hope alive, and look up
God loves you so very much.

There are tears, and there is pain
Love for each other still remains
Keep pressing on, looking up and not down
The love of God will still be found.

Velma R. Captain
Dallas, TX

Cool You Down Sometime

I feel your engine runnin' hard,
You're revvin' way too fast.
If I'm drivin' you home tonight,
Then I want you to last.
Don't want you to overheat,
It may make my motor blow,
And if we're gonna keep this pace,
Then we're gonna have to slow.
I'm feelin' the heat inside my ride,
Cylinders lubed and wet,
But I've got to cool down a bit
'Cause we ain't quite there just yet.
I've got this feelin' you're not that tired
And you could run all night,
And if you do, you'll still want more,
And I'll be drivin' till daylight.
This just may be the perfect match
As your gears scream and whine,
But for me to drive for years to come,
I've got to cool you down sometime.

Kurt T. Beck
Oakville, CT

Silent Tears

Alone they shed their silent tears
In a life that ignores their fears
They wear their black and blue so well
They're locked inside their private hell
They don't understand what they do so wrong
They're bad, they're worthless—the list goes on
They crave so much for parental love
Instead, they tremble at the hand above
These tears they shed reflect their pains
Their blood, their burns—internal stains
Why don't we hear their desperate cry?
Love to them does not apply
They cannot run, they cannot win
When every move is deemed a sin
The broken bones, their body will heal
But safety and peace, they'll never feel
Their terror and pain, they must not tell
They sit alone inside their hell
They fight so hard to be set free
But for their prison, there is no key. . . .

Pamela J. Proehl
Redmond, WA

Heaven's Gate

Take me back, my love, to Heaven's gate
Forgive me, don't forget me, I swear it's not too late.
Do you remember the days?
Lazy, sweet, in the summer haze?
Just you and I, hours flitting by
The only sound, your sweet sigh.
We would swim in the brook neath Heaven's Gate
Till the sun hung low and it grew late.
Riding home, I'd whisper to you
My love, my love, I will be true.
Promises broken, hearts bowed,
Is a second chance for love allowed?
Come back to me, my love, to Heaven's gate
Prove my penance to you isn't too late.
I will wait for you till night is falling.
Please, my love, let me hear your sweet voice calling.

At Heaven's gate . . . at Heaven's gate . . .

Jason M. Luttgens
Elizabeth, NJ

When I was a child, I wasn't sure what I wanted to be, but there was always a spirit within me, struggling to get out, struggling for control. Sometimes it seemed more demon than spirit. When I was young, I could not bring it under control and it would move and force me to write many things, some good, some not so good. I hope this work, "Heaven's Gate," may make some remember their past loves or seek new ones and to remember forgiveness is at the heart of love.

Metered Vices, Hail!

Your voice with clear locution rings
Each time your readings resonate
Another story's dim tractate.
Dimmed only, though, in doubt
It drafts some far-flung note that sings.
Nor do I mean to always pout
That thespians have died among
The common ranks. King James was wrong;
That Shakespeare's work is lost,
And words again will never shout
Or dance—from off the Earth be tossed
To cleave the highest sun in two
And color cloudy skies a blue!
But would I sheathe my sword
Up from the "tongues of Pentecost"

I should more darkly grieve the word.

Victor A. Schmidt
Sitka, AK

A local writer friend would mock or tease me at scheduled readings about my poetry being always in metered and rhymed mode. His poems were always absent these qualities, being in free verse. I soon saw the worth of making a "clubby" and cordial exercise from this (since he was quite persistent with it) by exchanging poems of friendly but hinted critique of each other's styles . . . a kind of back and forth "chatter," if you will. "Metered Vices, Hail!" was the first in "the series." But alas, sadly, his physical demise soon followed, as did my plan.

Who Will Wear the Crown?

Who will be the victor?
Who will wear the crown?
Who will be left standing
On the bloody battleground?

Who will be left friendless?
Who will fall from grace?
Who will leave his youth behind
When death stares in his face?

Who will pierce the shield wall?
Who will hold the line?
Who will bear the burden
Of souls lost in their prime?

Who will wave the banner
Of a king lost to a spell?
Who will take the glory
And the painful stories tell?

Barbara E. Selby
Waycross, GA

The Sounds of Sorrow

Death and destruction came
But not from the skies
No time for I love you
No time for goodbyes

The ground, it did tremble
Houses and buildings did fall
Not much time to think
No time to call

The sounds of their cries
Did pierce the air
There was death and destruction
Just everywhere

Some were buried beneath rubble
In a place dark as night
Would they be rescued
To again see the light

Their sounds of sorrow
Drift up into the sky
As they cry out to God
Our Father on high

We must hurry to help them
There is no time to wait
We must hear their cries
Before it is too late

Maggie E. Preece
Cameron, TX

To Sir Richard Francis Burton (1812–1890)

You unrolled your Persian carpet,
revealing a costly path.
Your verses fired my girlhood dreams
with songs of distant lands.
Around me, prosaic voices tutted,
"Women should stay home where they belong,"
You lifted the skirts of the East with your *Kama Sutra*.
Your *Arabian Nights* leaked musk in my sheets,
spreading oil on proper, well-bred lips
with your broad pen. Your wild exploits inflamed me.
Where you have gone, I would go also,
even to the source of the Nile,
but "No nice woman travels alone."

The price is worth the ruby, the cost is life.
Freedom brings the greatest risk. Alone
I travel; "no nice woman." Your courage drew me out.
My harem door you opened to nights of the Levant,
till dawn outlined the minaret,
and my eyes were filled with doves.
In Samarkand, a Stranger waits;
my guide when I go forth.
You Sufi heartthrob, Richard, Sir,
see how your dauntless quest
unrolled the Persian carpet
with the pattern of my fate.

Barbara M. Annan
Fairbanks, AK

Haiti Is Calling You

Haiti is calling you
Pleading cries for help
Somber tears are flowing
Every place the earthquake was felt.

This is a time of need
It's so hard to be alone
Heavy hearts dealing with grief
4:53 p.m. alive—4:54 p.m., gone.

Do you feel their pain?
No water and no home
Massive graves overflow
Darkness utters a hurtful groan.

Mothers lost sons and sons lost mothers
Smoke and dust were everywhere
Fathers lost daughters and daughters lost fathers
It all seemed so strangely unfair.

People gathered in the streets
Professing their faith with songs
Praising God for all their blessings
We still believe and we still belong.

The birds just don't sing anymore
There is wailing for the dead
Hope is leading them forward
It will take years to progress ahead.

Haitians shall survive this oppression
Love of God will be our mission.

Shirley J. Ottman
Sheboygan Falls, WI

Timeless Torment

Timeless teardrops fall with dismay,
Hopeless banters as I pray.
Seemingless thoughts of yesterday and today,
Moonlit silhouettes dancing on a hardened shallow bay.

Angie Jablonski
Plymouth, IN

Storms in My Life

Sometimes I go through storms in my life
God knows my heart and knows my strife
I feel the turmoil inside of me
Only I know it's there and God can see
I want to cry out to ease my pain
I feel as if I am going insane
I talk to God in Heaven above
God fills my heart with His unconditional love
In times of pain the first thing I do
I go to God in prayer because He feels my pain too
I think the storms will forever come
There will be many and then some
It's God's way of allowing me to see
His will is the way and only He can set me free

Vanessa E. Stewart
Anniston, AL

Only a Parent Knows

To all parents that know the grief of losing a child

Yesterday, we brought you home,
small and smelling of baby lotion and milk,
a scent only a parent knows and loves.

Yesterday, we brought you home,
laughing at the day's adventures,
a remembrance only a parent keeps and loves.

Yesterday, we brought you home
for the last time,
praying they made a mistake,
praying it wasn't you,
a pain only a parent knows
through the death of their child.

Yesterday, we brought you home,
and then we died.

Cora J. Fazio
Fairmont, WV

Looking into the Mirror

When I look into the mirror, my reflection, I do not know.

Whatever happened to that reflection I used to know,
The one I grew up with not so long ago?

Does the body just grow old, trapping the dreams of the youth
inside?

But I ask again; I feel the same,
My looks have only changed.
The me I see is simply not the me I used to be.

Thank God above we have our memories,
For without them, that reflection that I see
Could quite possibly be the end of me.

Hold on tight, remember your dreams,
Forget not your memories, for they will always
Let you see the me we used to be.

Cheryl A. Wilson
Clarksburg, WV

My Love

It grows and grows as each day goes by,
I'm so blessed and that is why
As time moves on, our love does, too.
I'm so thankful for a man like you.

Our love has grown from the start,
I love you with all my heart.
I think of all our times together,
It just gets better and better.

My love for you is deep.
Sometimes I can't even sleep.
I think of you day and night,
And can't wait till morning's light.

To be with you all day long,
Gardening, cooking, fishing, too.
I don't know what I would do
If I had to live without you.

My love for you is strong,
It just keeps going on and on.
You kiss me and hold me tight,
I love you will all my might.
Your warmth and loving, caring ways
Are engraved in my heart to stay.

I love you and you love me,
That's the way it will always be.

Barbara K. Layman
Miamisburg, OH

The Meaning of Friendship

What does it mean to have a friend
More stable than having a lover,
One person with whom to discover
Life's values that never end?
What does it mean to have a friend
To hold you in highest esteem
When shattered lies every dream,
And strivings in failures end?
A friend always helps you to measure
And brings to you special insight
To grasp the puzzles of life
In both disappointment and pleasure,
To separate darkness from light,
And triumph over strife.

Billie C. Davis
Springfield, MO

I was born in 1923 in Grants Pass, Oregon, while my migrant-worker parents were there picking hops. I am known in educational circles as the "hobo kid" because of an article in *The Saturday Evening Post* that was used by the National Education Association for a film *A Desk for Billie*. The film has been an inspiration to many teachers and is now available on DVD. Out in the fields, early in the morning, I was inspired to make up little songs. From that point of view, I have always been a "poet," and now in my old age, I want to share the delight of putting a soul into words.

The Mermaid

I was walking along the beach at noonday
for no particular reason, just a casual stroll.
I often take walks by the beach, the fresh air and rolling surf
take my mind off the darkness, the loneliness within my soul.
One day, as I walked along the oyster-ridden sandy turf,
I saw a young woman in the water, head and shoulders
bobbing just above the surf.
Though I'd never seen this pretty young woman before,
she called me by name and waved, so I invited her to come ashore.
She smiled and said she'd like to honor my request,
and although she said she wasn't afraid,
she said she couldn't come out of the water,
because she was what I'd call a mermaid.
At first I thought she was making a joke,
as many people like to do as kids in their youth,
but on entering the water and inspecting her a little more closely,
I found she wasn't kidding. She was telling the truth.
This mermaid named Amber said she had seen me walk the beach
many times, sometimes happy, sometimes sad,
but always alone and apart.
Amber said she decided to come to the surface
to comfort my soul, to relieve the pain in my heart.
For many days thereafter, even many weeks,
Amber met me at noonday along the little patch of beach.
Amber filled my heart with wonder;
she raised my soul to heights I thought I could never reach.
Then came the day I shall always regret.
Amber said she sensed I wanted her to join me
in my world indefinitely.
Of course, that could never happen, that could never be.
Amber said her time had come;
she accomplished what she wanted to do.
Amber said that she had to leave, but she told me, quote,
"I'll always love you."
With a mournful wave of her hand,
and a long meaningful look at me,
Amber submerged and vanished into the deep blue sea.

Alan D. Knight
Champaign, IL

I Lived to See

History is made every day
and it is made to stay
to remember how it was done.
I lived to see
a Black American president.
Another decade of history
almost sounds like a mystery,
but really it is for people to see
our God is still in control.
The world needs a change,
a change for the better.
He promised this change
to make the world better.
History was made for me
at eighty-three;
I lived to see.
Praise the Lord!

Marcella Neal
Brooklyn, NY

I am a matured elderly woman. I love music of all types, writing, and my love for people has always been strong. I was a nurse for thirty-five years and worked with people from every walk of life. I have three children. I have been writing for twenty years or more. My poems are religious and I give a message from the heart with God's love, courage, and faith. I am still writing and hoping every day to have some of my poetry published.

The Rocks, the Sand, and Me

The rocks are heavy,
Sunken in the earth,
Needing rain, wind, or Man
To move them from their birth.

Rocks are solid,
Yet they split;
I am a rock,
I must admit.

The sands are wanderers,
That always change,
They drift and move
And rearrange.

The sand makes castles,
Homes, and rocks.
I am the sand
That takes the knocks.

Marianne Bilicki Remishofsky
Colonia, NJ

Born in Bayonne, New Jersey, I have two poetically endowed sisters. My dad inspired my poetry writing, as during my childhood, he bought scenic poetry books and selected meaningful greeting cards for our mom, who also encouraged my poetry writing, which began at age eight. I am married and have a wonderful daughter, Meredith, and two grandsons, Andrew and Alexander. A retired teacher, I have a bachelor's degree in French with teaching certificates in French, Russian, and English, and some graduate work. This poem suggests that both deep-rooted strength and flexibility are necessities of personal survival in fulfilling one's dreams.

Echoes of Hurt!

Echoes of hurt flow from mountaintops to valleys below,
Overflowing into city walls.

Echoes of hurt flowed from the Twin Towers
As they fell into a pile of rubble.

Echoes of hurt were heard by families, friends,
And from nations around the world.

People listened for echoes of the Twin Towers of rubble
In hope of a voice from someone who may be still alive.

Echoes of hurt flow from city walls to valleys
To mountaintops, leaving memories of all
Witnesses to the falling of the Twin Towers on
September 11, 2001.

Carol A. Miller
Washingtonville, NY

I started writing poetry at the age of fifty-three and still love writing about the Lord
and Savior Jesus Christ. I've lived in New York City all my life. I remember
as a young girl riding the Staten Island Ferry, especially at night, and seeing the
awesome skyline of all the skyscrapers, although the Twin Towers were not known
then, except by native New Yorkers who would understand their beauty. I have been
married almost forty-eight years. We have five beautiful daughters, two who have
served in the U.S. Army, twenty grandchildren, and ten great-grandchildren.

A Sea That Has No Shore

Can a thought be capable of fire
When it burns inside my head?
Can it heat the embers it's stirring
That were left to die instead?

Immortality did not come by chance,
But endured in written words.
When the fire of an idea was lit,
It blazed in the minds that heard.

Let not the candle that lights a dark room
Melt away and be no more.
I will not lead an idle thought astray
To a sea that has no shore.

George J. Carroll
Levittown, NY

My Sister Lilly

A broken heart is what she had
Only wanting to be loved
No more pain
No more sorrow
With a smile of her face
She's at peace
She's an angel in Heaven.

Esther Fasfeld
New Rochelle, NY

The Tear

A little drop of water fell from her eyes.
To some, it was just a casual thing,
But to me, that drop of salty water
Was a powerful thing,
For it could reveal the inner person.
Enclosed in it were her deepest emotions,
All her thoughts and feelings
That are intangible to the outside world.
Inside that teardrop was crammed
Every love, every hurt of her life.
It was so precious and meaningful,
For it exhibited her concealed emotions.

Carolyn L. Perri
Plainville, CT

Chil'n-n-Ole Folk (A Southern Spiritual)

I hear the chil'n a-callin'.
They's lookin' for some joy
'Cause this ole world a-fallin'
Like some ole broken toy.

I's feelin' for the ole folk.
I know how hard they works
'Cause this ole world a-changin'
As death for them still lurks.

I hear the chil'n a-cryin'
'Cause Mama's been so mad.
I see the ole folk a-dyin'.
They's really feelin' sad.

My heart a-hangin' low, so low.
It really done all it could.
If e'er it come way up high,
It be for somepin' good.

Brian R. Oyler
Woodstock, IL

New Friends

Look around and make new friends,
They, too, know heartache, help make amends.
A smile, a hug, or a bouquet of flowers,
A rainbow—myth's pot of gold after the showers.

Life's a series of hopes and dreams,
Accomplishments create rivers out of little streams.
At the end, a special friend may be close by.
Don't close a door; listen, think, respond, try.

Reach out, remember what friendship is all about.
Caring, sharing, uplifting, erasing doubt.
In old age, a lifetime of dreams marching on,
Time to reflect, smile, and share as our pathway is trod.
Thankfully! Stress is less!
And for that, we thank God!

Elsie Stowell Raymond
Roseville, CA

An Angel

Flashes like the lighting
That brightens up the sky
Like the moon that has eyes.
Looking down from upon high,
Angels are God's messenger,
One who whispers in your ear,
Gives you a peaceful feeling
Of only good news you wish to hear.
One who is like the dewdrops
After it comes a pouring down rain
That comes to heal you,
Relieves you of illness and pain.
You bring us a blessing
Sent down from Heaven above.
Unimaginable how God's grace
Is filled with His precious love.

Nancy Lee Armstrong
Pulaski, VA

A Banner Bides a Dawn

Oh, once a fort prevailed a night
As banner hailed by early light
And 'firmed an earlier day of fight
When rightness strove 'gainst lordly might
With willingness ere death to go
Through hunger, want, and bloodied snow
Till last endure gained liberty
Neath ramparts of life's dignity.

Then fathers of a land so raw
Forged a code of founding law
To raise a better house to stand
For all who toil with mind and hand.

So when there ever breaks the day
That spirit is Man's guiding way
With readiness toward all in need
And aim above the mire of greed.

Then to flag this land of ours
Let ensign stars meld stripes and bars
To herald long as banners wave
A realm of free and true of brave.

Richard A. Spellerberg
Girard, IL

9/11/01

The land of the free,
our land of liberty.
Terrorists struck
our nation on 9/11/01.
This was so wrong.
Thousands of lives
were lost.
Our heroes!
Many perished at Ground Zero.
9/11/01, we must not
forget.
We will move forward.
yet...
The land of the free,
our land of liberty.

Pauline E. Blagrove
San Antonio, TX

To Heir

Riding through the country
Embracing rolling emerald fields
Knowing in the fall
Farmers harvest all the yields

Across this majestic country
Above fluffy cotton seas
Observing quilt patch areas
This sight, my memories eased

To sun-scorched sands of Vegas
With chance to feed the slots
My mind reflects in memories
Of accomplishments I sought

Among the many poets
So embellished with soul and speech
We mingled and we listened
With recognition we did reach

Judith M. McKillip
Iowa City, IA

I was born and raised in Iowa with heartfelt love for the country and the beauty of
the United States of America, which inspires my thoughts for poetry.

The Gifts

From the fires of creation
There came forth the gift of light
Stars to light the worlds around them
In their endless circling flight

From the turmoil of Earth's waters
There came forth the gift of life
Full of promise, full of purpose
Full of vigor, thrive, and strife

For the many varied life forms
There were many gifts for sensing
Gifts of touch and gifts of hearing
Gifts of taste and smell and sight

There came gifts of thought and language
There came gifts of art and music
There came gifts of faith and hope
And the greatest gift of all
That great gift that we call . . . love

Anthony Placeres
Los Angeles, CA

As an observer and seeker of knowledge living as a human on Planet Earth, I have learned from many sources about the wonders of the universe, the physical wonders that include the astrological and the biological, and the non-physical wonders from which our spirituality arises. I have found so many things that we are given that cannot be sold or bought; from the particles that make our existence possible to what we are capable of giving each other freely: respect, consideration, understanding, comforting, kindness, love. Things we should acknowledge and receive with gratitude. Gifts.

Caring

God made us to love one another
As we all are sisters and brothers
Your race, color, and creed
Should not stay here in greed
Not hate, disgust, and distrust
Our love, caring, and giving is a must
Our hearts and love to share
That's how we all should care
So let's all pull together to make our world better
Come, let's all hold hands
And show we can nicely band
Peaceful, lovingly, and caring
To show God's love that comes from above
The love God gave us to know
His love He gave us to show
To care and help everyone here
Far away or even near
Not one-sided love that God teaches us
So show Him we learned to be just
And hope it continues each day
Love can help us in every way

Esther L. Benton
Cincinnati, OH

I have four sons, Charles, Raymond, Robert, and Thomas (deceased sixteen years).
I have nine grandchildren, nine great-grandchildren, and I am eighty-two years old.
I make items for decorations like plastic angels, bird cages, and many other things.
I try to be nice and helpful to all who live here at the chateau. I enjoy all the items
like bingo and other games here. That's about it. I enjoy people. My husband died
sixteen years ago.

Mom or Mom

Is it by chance that "mom" spelled backwards is the same?
I think not, I muse
I choose to think it came to be by design
Who first uttered this moniker of love wanted no spelling error
A sacred name embodying indescribable devotion
Three letters seem inadequate on paper
But no, the trio tugs at the heart and elicits
Almost a universal image—love and sacrifice personified
Few words can evoke this, I ponder
How does a hundred-pound frail and dying woman
Handle this burden?
Profoundly and proudly, of course!
How could she be gone—who will replace her?
The weighty word has become ethereal
I can utter it no more
How fitting and ironic that three months later,
Her stone is still not inscribed; "No time," he moans
For truly, there is no date of demise; Mom
Will never pass away in my heart.

Christine Eagen
Poughkeepsie, NY

What Is a Marriage?

Please, would someone please tell me just
what a marriage is truly supposed to be like,
for I have yet to find out just what is a marriage.
It has been a good nineteen years and counting,
and I still have not figured out what in the heck is
going on with this woman
I have vowed to love, honor, and protect,
when most of the time, I feel that I am
the one who needs to be protected.
Will someone please tell me just what is a marriage?
Now I have learned over the years
who really wears the pants in the family.
What I mean, of course, is that it's no more
mine or me, me, it's ours or nobody's at all.
What I have found out in this two-way street
is that a woman's love is like none other
that any one man can imagine alone.
So tell me just what is a marriage?
It's not me anymore like it was when we first got together.
She was always there for me, no matter what,
but now, oh, no, don't even think about it.
She has time when it's on her terms.
Now it's your turn to shake the tree limbs.
You have to do a very good job at it or else.
So will someone please tell me what is a marriage?
I've been trying to find out by putting my best foot forward
and still I am coming up short in all,
and despite what has been said, we men still would like to know
that we are and will always put God first,
wife second, and all others last.
What is a marriage, please!

Charles J. Day Jr.
Glendale, AZ

Memories

Make every day a pleasant one
With memories that will be remembered always
Think of all the memories we have of the past
Memories shared are blessings that keep on giving
Use happy thoughts of all good days gone by
They were times that were wonderful
We never thought they would end
Now it seems so long ago
Let yesterday be and look what tomorrow will be
After all, we have only one life to live
Let's make what is left be a good life
We have tomorrow to deal with, there are many good days left
There's a silver lining in the days to come
This is something to look forward to
After all, we can't live forever, but there's no harm in hoping
So let's keep those memories in our hearts and minds
Tomorrow's memories will be in coming years
Let's hope for more wonderful memories with a silver lining
For many years to come with many wonderful memories

Donald W. Hunter
Casa Grande, AZ

Fading Thoughts

Gazing at the flowers plucked from yesterday
Lie dying in the heat of the sun
With each minute of each day
As they wilt in time, so does our love
Each time you don't say the words,
They lie dying beneath your skin
Lie dying as the flowers in the sun
As the flowers wilt in time does our love wilt away each time
Fading away as the flowers plucked to lie—to die in the sun!
Gazing at the flowers from yesterday!

Connie A. Miller
Waverly, NY

Chocolate Lover

Chocolate is my favorite candy.
It makes me happy, fine, and dandy.
A chocoholic I am.
I eat it as often as I can.
I have a sweet tooth,
Which started in my youth.
C-H-O-C-O-L-A-T-E,
Oh, I love thee!
Calories added up for years,
But at my age, who cares?

Irene Ashery
Delmar, NY

Seek His Face with Patience

We pray to God each day with care
With faith we know that God is there!
We might think that it's out of sight
But He answers us when the time is right.

We long to hear His voice divine
And see His garments oh, so fine.
His eyes, His hair, and smiling face,
The Lord of love and amazing grace.

To kiss His hand would be so sweet
Or rubbing oil on His feet.
To hug Him, this my love would show
But then I might not let Him go.

Lord on high in the holy place
Someday we'll see Him face to face
And kneel before the Heavenly Host,
Our Father, Son, and Holy Ghost!

For now I'll pray and with patience wait
To someday meet Him at the gate.
And when it happens, bells will chime
When God says, "Come, son, now is the time."

Donald B. Perlinger
North Huntingdon, PA

Calliope

You've been gone, my muse, a while
Had pestered me in my sleep
Even sacred naptime peeps!
Whispered in my ear your veil's
No peace, just poems are my trials
Pen and paper castle keeps
Ever onward time does creep
Ink I've written, miles on miles

I write for living now
It's second nature to me
I live for writing now
It's life and breath somehow
Poetry is nature's tome!
It's part of me now.

Darres J. Munds
Yountville, CA

It Began with a Flirt

It all began with a flirt . . .
A simple "I would like to talk to you"
Was all it took;
Before I knew it, I was hooked.
The language was so new to me.
You laughed at how innocent I could be.

It all began with a flirt. . . .
Your words touched me so.
I couldn't believe someone so far
Could feel so near.
The words you spoke made me blush,
Making me long for you oh, so much.

It began with a flirt. . . .
Send me a photo, who could it hurt?
Tell me your heart's desire, and I'll tell you mine.
I promise not to play with your emotions,
I promise to never make you cry.
It all started with a flirt. . . .
In the end, I did get hurt.

Stephanie M. Fletcher
Coram, NY

A Mother's Love

Mothers are the ones who give us life
Mothers take care of our every need
Mothers guide our childhood years
Mothers guide our teenage years
Mothers guide us during our adult years
They tend to feel that her job is finished
We forget mothers, that they have feelings, too
Do not forget, a mother's guidance is needed
It's not till they are gone
We really learn what a mother's love is
God, please take care of her
My mother is with You, God
I miss her so
The laughs, talks, and quiet times we shared
God, please give the love she needs
Like the love she gave all of us
Till I come to Heaven
Then I can take care of her again
Then she will know
What a daughter's love truly is

Joan F. Yiannitsis
Corona, NY

Flowers

What's more beautiful
Than a flower
As it thrives happily
In its favorite bower.
It dances gaily on a slender stem,
And needs no stitches
On its dress or hem.

It shares its nectar
With hungry bees,
And decorates the spreading trees.
Its petals vary in color and hue,
And are exquisite in red, white, or blue.

We can smell its fragrance
Everywhere as it spreads
Generously through the air.
"Wondrous flowers, tiny or tall,
You're beautiful in winter, spring, summer, or fall!

Maria E. Herbert
Lead, SD

Hello, My Beautiful Daughter

Hello, my beautiful daughter,
Welcome to my world.
With a husband and three sons,
I was glad to see a girl.

For weeks I didn't believe it,
Not even with my eyes,
Until each time I changed you,
And could see it wasn't a lie.

Your father handled you so carefully,
As if you could be broken.
Your brothers protected you so sweetly
With love that was unspoken.

You are a married woman now,
With children of your own,
But stress is ever present,
And your health is left unknown.

And now my beautiful daughter
Is trying to be a good wife.
She put trust into her husband,
And it may have cost her life.

Sheila D. Hylton
Indianapolis, IN

My children, grandchildren, father, mother, stepfather, brothers, and sisters are all an inspiration for my poetry. Life's experiences make up the rest. I have either lived it or watched things as they happen. I hope you enjoy this poem and look me up to read more of my poetry.

Our Precious Time

It's the greatest foe to all of mankind
Our losing battle, no answer to find
We play with our days, ignore them quite clear
Can't hear the tick-tock that rings in our ear
The life forms we live, days, hours, and years
Bring us emotions, happiness or tears
We live for the present, our future is now
Loving each blessing that time will allow
Lives have a schedule the second they're born
Some splendored with length or shortened with scorn
Regardless of woe or glorious way
Time continues on, has its final say
Same goes with nature, the rose or the tree
There's a time to bud and a time to be
To bloom with fragrance and reach for the sky
A time to be proud, then a time to die
So we are mere pawns as time walks its road
While we spend each day in our world abode
Our clock ticks our life, like sand through a sieve
Just when will it stop, have no more to give
We cannot escape, time sets its own time
When we leave the clouds, when we lose our prime
Mark well your moment, hold precious your day
Live full your lifetime till time flies away

Frank X. Hundshamer
Carlsbad, CA

The Lord above has given me ample time to enjoy the gifts of having four children and sixteen grandchildren. In addition, He has presented me with the time to come safely home from two wars and to cherish the pleasures of a good wife and family. He has allotted me a goodly amount of adequate time. That inspired this poem, "Our Precious Time." Time is indeed a gift and must be used wisely.

Memories Within

Your name is still a whisper on my lips
as at night I fall to sleep.
Lying with your shirt pressed close,
the memories make me weep.
Never in this world
had I been so full of life.
You romanced me with the stars
I was going to be your wife.
You were strong, but yet so gentle,
every touch filled with such care.
Whether at my best or at my worst,
unwavering, you were always there.
How can I explain to everyone
that your heartbeat alone sustained me,
your arms around me, holding me close,
was all I needed to make me happy?
I lay here in the darkness of my room
as my thoughts wander through the night,
so lost that I fear nothing can save me,
yet still I search for your light.
One day, I hope to see you again;
for now, I hold the memories tight.
Just know my life with you is all I dream of
every second of every single night.

Rachel-Marie F. Dolly
Bristol, TN

Quiet Grace

I believe
In the beauty of quiet grace
The sunshine through the sunlit curtain's lace
The warmth and beauty that just lights up someone's face

I believe in the beginning, in the artist's trace
Which becomes the beauty of such quiet grace

When you know enough
When you know when to be quiet
When you know how to have such grace
When you know where you fit
Where is your place

You understand the realm of quiet grace

How restful your face
You understand your case
The sanctity of your space
Within the world of silent, quiet, serene grace

Accept the inevitability of quiet chase
To work towards understanding of the beauty
Of
Quiet grace

Joy R. Wimer
Dublin, CA

How Do We Measure a Life?

As God loves the sparrow, so too, He loves children.
When a life is lost, we wonder about the meaning.
Faith reminds us that there is a truer purpose than we realize.
Years are not the measure by which a life is judged.
Innocence of a little child provides the immortality.
His life inspires all with enduring, purposeful passion.
Such mighty courage to fight with the happiest of smiles.
The duty of a life lived well has been fulfilled.
Years and decades hence will prove the great purpose.
His spirit lives in each of us as his lasting gift.
It was a chosen destiny reached so soon, but reached.
He suffers no more and is playing by God's feet.
Healing after mourning, but quiet healing still.
The sapling, then, is mightier than the oak.
Have faith in the love for him that has no ending.
Find peace knowing this tiny life had tall purpose.
One day we will all recognize the beauty of his testimony.

Eric A. Kreuter
Yorktown Heights, NY

This poem is dedicated to the life of Colin, a two-year-old boy who died of brain cancer. I was genuinely touched by the love and support of Colin's family and friends who stood by the family during Colin's treatment and attended the memorial service. As a poet, writer, and artist, I am inspired by the lives of others and the inherent beauty of God's creation. As Colin's wonderful family mourns, the lasting memory of Colin will eternally inspire. Thus, the immutable awe of the life of a small boy will always exist in the hearts and minds of others.

America Was Born in Violence

I say that America was born in many ways.
She was born on the plantations
where slavery was institutionalized
and where eventually Jim Crow took over the south.
She was born on the plains of the west
where genocide prevailed against the indigenous population.
She was born on the exploitation of the Chinese workers
who helped to build the Transcontinental Railroad.
She was born in the conquest of lands
from the Mexicans and the Spaniards.
She was born in the violence of death squads
whose leaders graduated from the American War College.
She was born when we allowed Indonesia to invade East Timor
and when we landed marines in Siberia to fight the Bolsheviks.

America has been born in blood and iron,
but there has always been the dream of a nation
which has struggled for peace and human rights
and has wanted to do what is right.
This can be a reality, if we, as a nation,
not make the cornerstone of our national policy
military might!

Allan S. Mohl
Scarborough, NY

I am a licensed clinical social worker who is semi-retired. My office is in Dobbs
Ferry, New York. I am married and have three adult children and five grandchildren.
My first published poem, "Two Questions: A Matter of Philosophy," was published
in 1997. Since then, I have written many poems and several have been published
in various anthologies. Many can be viewed online. Currently, I am a member of
the Hudson River Writers' Center and the Academy of American Poets. My poems
are based on observations, feelings, and life experiences. They reflect my eclectic
interest in music, history, science, politics, and human behavior.

Nadia's Need for Him

Looking back,
It was naivete and sheer stupidity
That had me convinced
He loved me.
His ease in asking me for money,
The way he kept "us" a secret,
The reasons he would invent
To keep him from calling me
"His girl,"
And his using me as a refuge
When he fell out with "her."
However, none of that mattered,
Especially when I realized
I was head over heels.
And him,
He treated me
As if I'd always be there.
I, too, believed it,
But the day I knew
We were over
Was when he called out her name,
And didn't care
That I had suddenly
Died.

Latonya D. Sanders
Compton, CA

The Fog

The fog envelops me,
Or is it my ambiguous dream that clouds reality?

I exist for nothing.
There is no one there.
Beauty is not mine.
No love to share.

Last to be chosen?
Perhaps not at all.
Always trying to climb,
Always succeeding to fall.

I walk through the misty night,
Cloaked in a veil of nothingness,
Mercifully hidden from embellishments
That have passed me by.

I walk from vagueness to insignificance,
And ask,
Why, God, why?

Corinne Dell'Aria-Hallett
Prescott, AZ

Sadness

Sadness
sometimes
I feel at
what could
have been,
lacking
understanding
of why,
puzzled by
events.

Kathy C. Langen
Rochester, NY

I was born August 2, 1946 in Buffalo, New York to Matthew and Elanor Cullen. I attended the university on a Regents Scholarship doing honors with Robert Creely, graduating from the State University of Buffalo in 1969. I am employed as a page in the business-social sciences division of Central Library of Rochester and Monroe County. I write regularly weekdays. Sometimes I write a poem. This poem was written this year where I live in Rochester, New York.

Life Is . . .

Life is about finding things that make you happy.
Whether that is love or money, it should be about you.
Life is stressful because nothing is easy.
There will be good days and bad days and days that are in between.
Life is about smiles and laughter, but not at someone else's expense.
By being selfish in life, you will get nowhere,
But by being generous and giving, you will go far.
Life is waking up knowing that someone loves you, no matter what.
By loving yourself, it allows you to love others.
Life would never be the same without the people you choose
To be part of your life; choose wisely.
Living life is not always easy, but it is fun anyways.
Live life to the fullest and love like you want to be loved.
If life was meant to be easy, then it would never end.

Kandy D. Cox
Florence, AZ

october loch lomond

turn softly softly turn
green gold to gold burn
trees billow autumn full
to bursting

while
lofting grey veil sky
soft fold and shadow high
curtain drapes on craggy hill
and heather

and
long loch foil sheening
gathers gold and sky gleaming
silver in its single eye
winking

as
spice wooded leaf sodden
fern fringed and moss boggen
shores sip the silver cup
of lomond

Barbara L. Nelson
Kenmore, NY

Ode to the Doctor

A ritual unto the living
Total server of life
Scientist examining well-being
Curing much physical strife
Mechanic for the body
Comforter to the ill
A doctor reaches out
Extending love and goodwill
With years and years of training
To fulfill a special dream
The doctor's education
Continues ream upon ream
Dedicated, understanding, and true
This wise doctor must be
He touches precious gifts
Given unto all humanity
Highest regards to the doctor,
A healer, counselor, and friend
Mankind has been blessed
Time after time again.

Barbara K. Demaree
N. Ft. Myers, FL

Mimi

I found you in a pet shop
Half-asleep on the top of
A swarming mass of kittens
A smile of contentment
On your little face
At finally reaching the top

I named you Mimi
For your voice could rival
Any soprano in *La Boheme*

Your favorite perch
The back of my easy chair
Happily bumping me
With your tail

As I watch you
Sleeping on my lap
I know that someday
You will grow old
And pass out of my life

But I will not
Think of that today

Dorothy M. O'Neal
Albuquerque, NM

All My Life

Since I was young, I needed to know
in this troubled world the way I should go.

This gift I was given could be the way,
but only time and effort could lead me I'd say.

People come and people go,
but the one's I love were there for me.
So with eyes of hope, my gift, they'd say,
would be my direction would be my way.

All my life I felt this true,
the ones I love, they really knew.
Now I stand before all of you,
through their eyes of faith and my life anew.

Look at me and really learn
that in an uncertain world, it's okay to yearn.

Let your life serve for you as a way to see
that if you have a gift, don't leave it be.

All my life, I always knew
that this gift I have would one day touch all of you.

Michael G. Zurl
Remsenburg, NY

Tropical Rain

Tropics, hot and steamy,
welcome the rains with open arms.
Humidity, heavy with earthy smells,
tall grasses begin to sway,
with trees picking up that rhythm.
Waiting, but not for long,
as the beating of the rain begins,
drowning out all sounds.
Lush tropical landscapes slowly disappear
behind a wall of water
that seems to have no beginning or end.
For only a few moments,
sounds, smells, and pressure become intense.
Then as the rain subsides,
steam begins to rise from the cooled earth,
water droplets trickle off the leaves.
Here and there, puddles
left behind as if they were
footprints from the rain.

Patricia M. Bisgrove
Brookings, OR

Jack the Barber

The barber comes to our house
Since my husband can't get out.
The barber hurt his Achilles heel,
So he's not up and about.

I decided I'd give the clippers a try,
And got it ready to go.
A little nervous, I started it up,
And boy, was I ever slow.

Around the bottom, things were fine
Until I started upward, it begun.
Then things got tough and way too short,
So I kept on going till done.

His hair is so short, I could cry,
It will all grow out, but when?
I hope the barber is well by then
So he can cut it nice again.

Well, Jack the barber is on the job,
And he works hard all day.
The hair on my husband is still too short,
So there's nothing more I can say.

Carol J. Meier
Freeport, IL

We have been married since 1952 and have four daughters, seven grandkids and twelve great-grandkids. My Husband has chronic obstructive pulmonary disease, and is unable to get out. Jack Grigsby has been Harold's barber for many years and comes to our house to cut his hair. It is a very kind gesture and certainly appreciated by us. We are thankful for such a wonderful friend. I dedicate this poem to Jack. Our daughters, Catherine, Donna, Diana, and Patricia enjoy my writings. I have been published ten times. God bless everyone.

He Still Leads

From humble beginnings
To humble endings
God had led my soul.

He showed me many things
In between, then saved me,
And made me whole.

All the lessons in between,
Were sometimes hard to bear,
But they were lessons with me, He shared.

I didn't walk the road alone
As I struggled through my life.
He went with me all the way.

And now that I am old and gray,
He still leads me on my way
Though all my struggles every day.

Mary G. Bognar
Buffalo, IA

Through many trials, God has always been there for me. When things look the darkest, God lets the light shine through. The best family God has given me is my church family. They always support me and stand by me. By putting my faith and trust in the Lord, God has given me seventy-nine years of joy and love.

Flickering Life and Starlight

The night was still
except for whimpers of a dying wind.

The shy North Star
peeked from behind passing clouds
and blinked to the lullaby
of an ebbing west wind.

A restlessness
prickly as pine needles
pierced my heart
as I sat under that canopy of stars,
instant reminders of flickering life.

For so it was on that night years ago
that the light of the star of my life,
my beloved, unexpectedly ebbed.

Then came silence.
In the warmth of the night,
I shivered.
My misty eyes looked upward
to the stars, now dimming,
as dark clouds, like a pall, enveloped all!

Ruth V. Fierros
Laredo, TX

So This Is Farm Life

There was a farm in Watervliet
That was said to be quite neat,
But for two little kids from Queens,
It really was not a treat.
If at night you had to go,
You would hold it all in until you busted,
Until enough courage you mustered.
You would walk through the door,
Believing you would return no more
And by now your face was all flustered.

Your milk came straight from the cow
You never had this before—oh, wow!
There were turnips and garden squash
We have to eat this? Oh, gosh!
There was flypaper over the table;
Why must if hang so low?
It rendered the flies unable,
Why it hung there, we will never know.

Oh, Mother dear, what have we done
To make you put us here?
We miss our friends and we miss you, too,
Please do not make us come back next year.

Carol R. Laino
Mineola, NY

The Blank Paper

I have a blank piece of paper which expresses no affection
until the words that are written down give it meaning and expression.
A blank piece of paper holds no knowledge of what is said,
but it holds a mystery to some of the things that may be read.
A blank piece of paper holds no clues or vision,
but we use it sometimes to make our choices and wise decisions.
A blank piece of paper can sometimes be a challenge and a test,
for it can hold the awards and gratitude of some one's great success.
A blank piece of paper is rewarding
if the knowledge and use for it are good.
It can tear down the strong walls
and rebuild a community's neighborhood.
A blank piece of paper can tell of the past and the future to come.
It tells of a revolution and an evolution of things yet undone.
A blank piece of paper says a little, but it can mean so much.
It's what's on that paper coming from the mind, touching the heart
in what we will trust.
A blank piece of paper is only blank
if what is said stays in our head.
Until God inspires our heart
can people begin to understand what's read.
A blank piece of paper has a great purpose
and a really exceptional meaning
if the wisdom and knowledge comes from those
who achieve their goals and keep on dreaming.
Though the paper may be blank, keep it in you heart.
The blank is the perfect and most rewarding way to start.

Joel Woods
Wichita, KS

How Hard Is It?

A fall from grace it does seem,
Letting go of everything I did know
To simply fall and just let go.
Of this and that, I do not need,
My past bound to repeat and see what I have seen.
The hurt, the pain, and all the tears I have shed,
I will no longer fall a victim to
The world's disgrace called love with two.
A heart to merge with mine I have chosen
To let you go and remain unfrozen.
Toward that edge I do walk blind,
Scared, yet eager to what I may find.
How hard is it to just let go?
A new path I have chosen,
A path to wander along alone,
No more lovers tangled in a mess of one.
My heart cries no and my head cried yes;
Letting go is causing more distress.
Yet the fall I have chosen and forward I will walk.
Alone along the path, it is here I have fought.
For once, for all, the deed is done
As tonight I fall into the black abyss of one.
How hard is it to just let go?

Christina M. Trerotola
E. Machias, ME

The Master Weaver

God's weaving out a tapestry, each Christian is the threads.
In His Word and with His Spirit, He guides us day by day.
No matter race or color, we're all equal in His eyes.
No matter which religious label, none of these applies.
He's the Master weaver, He knows just what He wants to do,
And when His portrait's finished,
It will be perfect through and through.

Sharon E. Kight
Oakland, MD

Missing You

Sunrays shining, window bright
Another day, another night
Feeling restless, feeling blue
Knowing my heart misses you
Eating at a table for one
Being alone, not much fun
This will have to be my life
'Cause I can't stop being your wife
Each day gets better, so I'm told
Time heals all, but not the soul
Looking for a new tomorrow
To change this hurt and heal this sorrow

Carol A. Sulak
Murrieta, CA

This England

Here in such endless beauty, England lies,
That green and pleasant land which fills the eyes
With meadows lining slowly moving streams
As those abroad remember in their dreams.

The lonely windmill turning empty sails
Looks down upon the fields below, and hails
The rising sun afire with golden ray
Sweeping the dew like tears from yesterday.

A weathered castle, silent by its moat,
Reviews the passing centuries as they float
In endless time before its ancient walls,
Which once knew kings and captains in its halls.

This island nation, once by Churchill led,
Paid for the price of freedom with its dead,
As it had done in days long gone before,
When Drake and Nelson manned the ships of war.

Tranquility, and all that it inspires
Now reigns across the countryside and shires
Its sandy beaches now in peace we roam,
This blessed kingdom, washed by waves of home.

John T. Saxon
Palm Springs, FL

Kindness

Embrace those whom you love
as each day starts anew,
be graceful in your actions
with all you say and do.
Judge not the hearts nearest
when unkindness they display,
let patience and forgiveness
be the message of today.
Never take for granted
a moment you can share,
or a chance to make clear
the depths of which you care.
For now our lives go forward,
but one day we'll cease to be,
what attributes shall I leave behind
for all the world to see?

Katherine E. Neblo
Gilbert, SC

Peace Poem

I am a river flowing to every lake and every pond not
leaving any to dry out.
There might be some sticks and stones through my
path holding me back, but I always make it through.
Lakes and ponds are always so happy when I give
then water equally because they can never have
enough; just as I quench the thirst of the many people
that live near.

Erika J. Lemieux
Essex Junction, VT

My Las Vegas

Landmarks, from the truly aesthetic to pathetic.
Art-forms, opulence, as well as downright tawdry.
Streaks of winning, but mostly losing performances.

Ventures, for those high-stake risks and hazards.
Experience, society at play.
Gamboling, gambling, and also your gadabouts.
Artificiality, but with a touch of pride.
Sweetness, at times, overwhelms the greed.

Natural, ingeniousness for unchecked originality.
Venture, chance at any table, unpredictable.

Andre Pigeon
Las Vegas, NV

Candy for the Angels

A little boy took sick while visiting his grandpa.
That night, an angel came to him in his dream.
She showed him Heaven.
I am the angel that is taking care of your little friends.
The next morning, he told his grandpa
what he had saw in his dream.
"I saw my friends, Billy Joe, Jimmy, and Ben, you remember him.
Red swings, in our park.
I want to go to Heaven. Take me there, Grandpa."
"I can't."
"Take me down to the candy store. I want to buy
some candy for the angels. They are taking care
of my friends up there."
He walked into the candy store. He said to the
lady there, "I want to buy some candy for the angels,
they are taking care of my friends up there.
I want some lollipops and some gummy bears,
and all of your jelly beans to send to the angels up there."
The little boy passed away, taking his candy with him.
So he, Billy Joe, and Jimmy are swinging
on Ben's red swings in Heaven's candy land.

Maggie V. DeHart
Delmar, MD

At the Brink

Disaster looms
In not so many moons.
How do we find strength
To go the full extent?
Where do we find love
To rise above?
The safety net unravels,
Disease, famine, intolerance all travel.
World thinkers are clearly baffled.
How could our world of
Beauty natural,
With quiet and calm pastoral,
Crumble into the dark night,
Creating horrific images of fright?
We live uneasy, we work insecure.
We pray in disbelief, we wait in waning hope.
We face huge bulwarks of pain,
Not understanding in the main.
Where do we go from here,
As we teeter on the rotting pier,
As we stand at the brink,
Terrified that we might sink
Into an abyss, a bottomless chasm?
Our world is in free-fall.
Evil is supreme overall.
Look up, look up,
Implore God's grace.
May His compassionate bounty
Enlighten our race.

Delores L. Staton
Stoughton, MA

The Learning Trip

I have sailed the seas of poetry,
The captain of my ship.
My cats have sailed the seas with me,
And I have learned on this long trip
How dear life is and yet how short
The time we spend together,
To use it wisely and our discoveries to savor.
I learned to respect each species
As they are uniquely each their own,
How to treat each one with love and care,
And to hold each one alone.
I learned that life is just the feelings
That each of us can feel,
And that all the rest does not matter,
As it is all quite unreal.
When I spot land, we will anchor
And bring this ship to port.
I will step onto this Earth better off
For what my mind has taught.
Be aware that life is spare,
And what you do, you do not rehearse,
And when our time is done here,
There are better things than Earth.

Jeanette F. Terry
Valley Park, MO

My Butterfly

Life, I see through a foggy, hazy mist.
My world is safe, secure, snug, and warm.
What need have I of the open sky?
Here, I am out of harm.
Wrapped in my cocoon, happiness is this!
Time passes, days, nights roll into one.
Is it me who is changing? My cocoon no longer fits.
"Your life is short," I heard my maker croon.
"Time to come out and leave your cocoon."
"But I am safe here," I procure.
"Out there, things are not secure."
"For giving you life, is this my just return,
That you'd choose to remain a worm?"
"For you, I chose a special role.
You are my pallet of colors, the toll
Of all that is beautiful to me, thee!
So spread your wings and fly—
Don't let life pass you by.
Your fulfillment of life has just begun.
You have but one day in the sun.
Count your blessings from me up above
That I gave you this one day to find joy and love.
As a worm, do you want to die
When you could be my butterfly?
Try, try, try, fly.
Live life, my butterfly."

Joan M. Lovendoski
Sicklerville, NJ

95

Through Nick's Eyes

You look at me
and register normal,
but I am different
in ways you cannot see.

I am an old soul
trapped in a young body.
I am a stranger
sometimes even to me.

But my heart still beats
and I have dreams that
through the eyes of one
without my afflictions,
they do not see.

I am a child of autism,
but I am a child who
loves and dreams and
dares to be me.

Linda M. Romano
Canonsburg, PA

My nephew, Nicholas, was the inspiration for my poem. Nick has high functioning autism, Asperger's syndrome. He is a unique and intelligent individual. My cousin, Christine, said, "On the day Nick was born, the souls of our ancestors collided into him." I like to think those souls were fighting to be a part of this wonderful boy. Nick is just scratching the surface of his talents. With the careful guidance of his parents and a school system that realizes that not all children should be taught in the same manner, Nick is destined to do great things.

My Mother

I remember when I was a small tot
Her hand was always there to guide me
She would sing to me as we sat by the fire
As I was growing up it was her soft voice
And spoken words that soothed my hurt

I have a mother who would sit and watch
Her children run and play
She would speak softy as we would cry
From the hurt from our games
Listen! Come and sit here with Mother

One day I got sick which I never understood
As I left with a nurse for the doctor
Mother, it was your smile and hug that
Kept my spirit up until I got back home
To her love, warmth, and comfort of home

For a mother's who more precious than words
Time has gone from a tot to a daughter
Who has a home of her own
My future you helped me build
From love, great memories, words of kindness
Bless you, Mother, from a daughter's love.

Bonnie R. Wright
Mountain City, TN

In 2004, I realized my love for writing was challenged when I had a chance to enter one of my poems in a contest. I won first place as amateur poet, a bronze medal and a silver bowl. My husband is my biggest fan. He is an artist. He told me, "Now it's your time to fulfill your dream." My family gave me the foundation to build on. I'm happy at the age of eighty years old to put my thoughts down on paper. My dreams are fulfilled, and I am happy.

Dear St. Michael

Dear St. Michael, prince of heavenly hosts,
Lead your faithful, guard our children most.
Send your angels down from Heaven,
Keep us safe within.
Dear St. Michael, guard us from all sin.

Dear St. Michael, keeper of the gate,
Prince of all the seas, your victory waits.
Keep us safe in every battle.
Evil seeks control.
We rebuke the ruin of our souls.

Evil is roaming and seeking to kill.
Dark are the spirits who do Satan's will.
Let God rebuke him, we do humbly pray.

Please defend our souls.
We'll fight to be whole.

Dear St. Michael, strength above us all,
Heal the sick, protect us when we fall.

Send your angels down from Heaven.
Keep us safe within.
Dear St Michael, guard us from all sin.

Palmira R. Turbetti-Motto
Stockton, CA

Palmira (Pam) Turbetti-Motto, a singer-songwriter from Stockton, California, has been immersed in music ministry for over ten years. She was originally inspired to write sacred poems during her vocation as music director at St. Michael's Church in Stockton. Palmira decided to return to higher learning and began to continue working on a degree in music after a twenty-year employment in banking. She is currently a music education major at the University of the Pacific in Stockton and continues to compose music in a variety of genres. Her principle instrument is voice. She enjoys teaching music privately and is currently working towards a bachelor's degree in music education.

This Endless Road

All my life, it seems I've been traveling down this endless road
Always letting the hand of Fate point the way ahead unknown
I won't apologize for all the stops I've made along the way
I can't change what's in the past, we can only live in what's today
Although the trip has been so long and weary, if I only knew
That my endless road would finally end when it made its way to you

Mitch Gross
Pompano Beach, FL

Continuity

Morning slips away
Blooming with sway
Into a midday
Lending afternoon's pay
To evening's delay
And forthcoming bay
Of night's music forte
Yielding softer bouquet
With peaceful assay
To a sun's ray
Bursting forth as
The new day.

Othella Brogan
Lincoln, AR

99

Lonely

Lonely is the person
Who lives from day to day,
Hoping that tomorrow
Will make him bright and gay.

Lonely is the life
Of a soul without a friend,
For who would care or worry
If his life would cease and end?

Lonely means forsaken
When you need someone so much.
A tender look, a sweet caress
Or just a loving touch.

Lonely, lonely, lonely
How does one cope with life
When all one really asks for
Is relief from stress and strife?

Some of us were born to give
And some were born to take.
The takers make roiled waters,
But the givers make no wake.

Mae Levaas
N. Fort Myers, FL

Coloring

In the colors between the trees
Floating with leaves
Following butterflies
Shadows of gold.
Remember beauty like this.
Take me where I am
With myself to the colors of me.

Marcie G. Slater
Frederic, MI

Color Within

I write in green.
I think in black.
I see in pink,
With blue flashbacks.
My orange blood,
My whitened thoughts,
My red heart flood,
My gray love sought.
Some purple tears,
Some see through skin,
Some yellow years,
Some color within.

Courtney J. Bope
Rushville, OH

Reflections of Surviving Motherhood

As I think back about raising my two boys,
All the love, laughter, frustration and joys,

I can see that I've certainly been blessed,
And I miss them; they've both left the nest.

Oh, there were times when I prayed for this day,
When I wished that they'd both "go away!"

But it was only the stresses as their mother
And the challenging times with one or the other.

The needed Dr. Spock book I tried hard to find,
One to help me cope with a teenager's mind!

But I decided that this "guide" wasn't to be
Because if some folks had read it, you see,

They might not have had their girls and boys,
And opted instead for vacations and toys.

Nancy L. Oswald
Gladstone, OR

I was born and raised in Oregon City, Oregon and blessed with thirty years of marriage to John Kent Oswald. I began writing poetry upon his death ten years ago. Many tearful nights I'd find myself at my computer typing lyrics as they spun through my head. We raised two sons, Jeffrey and Brandon, who provided us with many memorable years of parenting. Although we had many fun-filled days with them, there were a few times in between that brought frustration along with the joy. I've dedicated this poem to them to remind me I did survive motherhood.

The Lamplight

I hope that the lamplight in your heart
and the lamplight in your mind
never goes out, because the lamplight
that you bring into our existence
lights up the darkness in each of our lives.
Thank you.

Eddie G. Fernandez
Seattle, WA

Winter

Winter is setting in,
the whiteness of the snow,
blinding the eyes,
making quiet all common sounds.
It comes to make the Earth
look pure again,
showering the trees with her flakes,
freezing all water solid,
covering all colors,
showing only white to purify.
Winter has come once again
to do its cleaning.

John E. Shumaker Jr
Youngwood, PA

Pen and Ink Drawings

Flowers from inkwells grow
Butterflies flitting everywhere
Pussy willows mewing soft and low.

Inspiration from ink wells flow
Detracted by impudent crows
Hard to keep all your thoughts in a row.

Flowers in art galleries bloom
No perfume fills the musty room
Amid the clowns and red balloons.

Jane Pierritz
Chicago, IL

I am a senior citizen, ninety-four years old. I have written poetry most of my life. I am grateful to have this opportunity. I was accepted by Noble House and Poetry.com for several years and Sparrowgrass, now out. I won $300 and a chance at a book. I wish they hadn't folded, The International Library of Poetry. In my poem, I was thinking about how beautiful ink drawings are and how often people don't see this loveliness. They rush by, uncaring.

My Yellow Paper Dress

I picked up the paper and what did I see—
Something that was advertised just for me.
Something that I've wanted for a long, long time.
Now this special's only three dollars short a dime.

So I grabbed my purse and headed for the bus.
I wanted to get there ahead of the fuss.
They only had one in the color that I wanted,
And I bought it even though I knew I'd be taunted.

My very special dress ain't really too loud,
But wherever I go, it sure draws a crowd.
I'm invited to balls and every social affair.
If you hear of a party, rest assured, I'll be there.

Uptown, downtown, no matter where I go,
In my yellow paper dress, I'm the hit of the show.
East side, west side, all around the city,
In my yellow paper dress, I'm really quite pretty.

I never had a steady beau until I got that dress.
I've even had my picture taken by the local press.
I hope this won't end when my dress is worn and gone,
'Cause I can never get another at the old Bon Ton.

Douglas J. Shay
Taylorsville, UT

Silent Cry

Sirens screeching, screaming by,
In the corner, a little girl cries.
To herself she has to hide
The fear she feels inside.
She knows what's happening isn't right.
She knows her mother can't see the sight
Of what happens late at night.
Fear is all she knows and she doesn't want to be alone,
For if she tells, to the street she'd be thrown,
And her momma wouldn't love her anymore.
Silence is her secret and it festers inside her like a sore.
When did this all start, she doesn't know.
She can't exactly remember . . .
Maybe in the winter with the snow.
Once he came and got her at night.
He made her touch him, and she heard a noise so slight.
It was her momma coming up the hall.
She hid behind a chair curled up in a ball.
Being so very quiet, she made not a sound,
Crying to herself as she lay on the ground.
Seven years old, what could she do?
Who would believe what she was going through?

Stacy L. Campbell
Gretna, VA

The Devil's Game

You can't beat the devil
In any game
That you play.

You can try your heart out,
But it never turns out
That way.

The devil
Is a cheat and a liar,
And all that we are to him
Are mortal fools.
When you play with the devil,
You play by his rules.

Keep praying
To your Lord in Heaven,
And try and keep things cool.
Don't be the devil's party thing.
Instead, be the Lord's
Heavenly tool.

David L. DeVilleries
Los Angeles, CA

My birth date is January 31, 1947. I write about things that I have learned in my
life. Some of these things may keep me from going to Heaven. Old age is creeping
upon me, so I will write poems as long as I can. Still, no matter how good or bad
my work turns out, I will always be my number one fan.

Deleted?

Electronic devices
direct my thoughts.
My brain has become
a cell phone?
Text messages
soar in my mind
leaving episodes
to remember.

For reasons unknown,
they flicker out.
Somehow, the message
was deleted
on the cell phone
of my mind.

The battery must be weak
in my remote control.

Dolores R. Patitz
Glidden, WI

Dear Son

Life is cruel, unjust, and mean.
These are things that remain to be seen.

You think you're smart,
but your life has just begun,
and if you keep these lies up,
you'll find yourself on the run.

I don't say things to pick or be mean,
but remember,
these are things that my eyes have seen.

I've been down that road,
and I changed my ways,
but if you don't stop,
eventually you won't have a say.

Please, son, I beg you to be wary.
Don't pick a load that you can't carry,
and please, son, you're not that old.
The truth is that this life is just that cold.

Nicole L. Barkley
Springfield, OH

Blessings

Grey skies a-dawning,
Awaken to another day.
Where is you life going,
Where can happiness stay?

Place a hold on thoughts aflutter,
Calm your breath with a sigh.
On loved ones ponder,
Count your blessings, don't cry.

Blessings abound 'round every corner,
Every sweet flower and friend.
Each bring sunshine and laughter,
Messages of their love send.

Warm letters, frequent calls,
Neighbors cheery hails,
Birds singing, children's voices,
All an uplifting choir, it never fails.

For every tear, a smile,
For every smile, an opening heart.
Sunshine passed on, and in a while,
A new view and a new start.

Kathryn D. Bochantin
Glendale Heights, IL

Taking Charge of My Life

I am taking charge of myself,
so is it no surprise that I am taking charge of my life?
No longer satisfied am I with taking whatever you elect to give.
No! I will not cry, I am taking charge of my life.
I am now more vocal, I do have a voice, I demand my respect,
even if politically incorrect. Your forced, exerted strife,
no longer will you influence my thoughts. My past failures will not
be the basis of the conversation. I will acknowledge my
shortcomings at my own discretion. I am taking charge of my life,
I will be my own social system. I am a work of art, you see!
I've had a change of heart; I am taking charge of my life.
Sex is not the core of me; active or celibate, my choice it will be.
An irresistible force I now follow, stepping into my own shadow.
I am taking charge of my life, weaving magic in my efforts
to go beyond my emotions,
strengthening the bonds within my soul—I make this motion!
I am taking charge of my life,
I am the only reason for the responses which escape me.
I accept full responsibility.
All negative aspects I terminate,for forward I now accelerate
along this journey, a real relief.
While escaping you, I found me;
therefore, I am taking charge of my life.

Judy Johnson
Indianapolis, IN

These Hills

These hills used to echo with the beating of drums,
and the breezes all carried the young men's brave hums
as they marched from the village to fight for a cause,
over deep, churning oceans and off to the wars.

These trees in the forest once were splendid in green,
and the pathways well worn where the children had been.
The leaves now are scattered, the limbs go unclimbed;
searching each day for sunlight, they keep marking time.

These fruits in the gardens grow so quickly to seed
when absent the harvest of what villagers need.
The old men and the mothers and the babies alone
wait nearby that the ocean might carry youth home.

And perhaps on the morrow, full sails will appear
on the distant horizon, and heading for here,
soon they'll furl to reveal how the sojourners fared,
which ones were slaughtered and which ones were spared.

These hills that once glowed with the villagers' dreams
now lie hard by cold winds bearing heartbroken screams
of the people whose children went to fight for a cause,
and felt fully the folly of fighting in wars.

Joe A. Syiek
Huntington Beach, CA

Precious Child

Precious child, all this shame and pain,
your father disgracing his name.
Satan stealing your years.
Your father will never know all the tears.
Precious child, all alone and scared
in this sinful world that is shared.
Afraid of your father and his sinful way,
all you know to do is pray.
Precious child, praying all this shame and pain not to stay,
wishing your father would not be this way.
Satan laughing at what he's done,
not worrying about God and His Son.
Precious child, older and stronger,
knows what to do to be free from this sin any longer.
Your prayers were not in vain,
now your father knows your pain.
Precious child, no more to fear,
for God has wiped away all your tears.
No more shame and pain, precious child.

Tequila Brou
Colfax, LA

Shoelaces Tied in the Dark

Toe stubbed on steel-wheeled bedstead.
Shoelaces tied in the dark.
Never breakfast with the "spouse" unwed,
this dis-easy love hardly a lark.

Get out of my life, you louse,
my ocean of dreams is run dry.
I've given you all my love,
you nothing that money can't buy.

You've tied your shoes in the dark.
Now go before dawn shows how pitiable you are,
never again park your shoes on my floor—
shoes whose laces you will always tie in the dark.

Michael Granich
Berkeley, CA

My Prayer

Please God, don't take me yet, I love it here
With all the folk and friends I hold so dear.
Should I enumerate the joys
Of hearing laughing girls and boys,
Of sitting in a corner small
Holding the littlest of them all,
Or on a vastly grander scale
Watching the antics of a whale?
Then, what of birds and bees and trees
And flowers, too; yes, what of these?
I could go on and on, and then go on again
About the world I love so much, but then . . .
'Tis said Your world is wondrous to behold
With beauty, love, and joys as yet untold.
I'm sure one day I'll come to You and say,
Please take me home, I'm ready now to stay,
But please, oh, please, don't let it be today.

Leonie F. Nulle
Media, PA

A Moment of Silence

A moment of silence to a soldier's ear
Directs all his thoughts and feelings of fear
As the plane's door opens and he's ready to jump
His nerves are just rattled, his heart gives a jump
Lord, let my chute open is my prayer to You
And guide right beside me till this jump is through
As his boots touch the soft, still sand
He gently lets go of the "invisible hand"
Takes a deep sigh, wipes a tear from his eye
Looks up to Heaven, and whispers, God, You're a great guy

Patricia L. Carstens
Oak Forest, IL

A sharing of love in friendship to a wonderful Elk friend, Billy McGuire and his wife, Janice. They inspired me to write this poem. He is proud to be a paratrooper and the unselfish fears and joys he holds in his heart while serving his country were such a blessing, as was the sharing of this poem with others. A treasured friend he will always be, not only in "A Moment of Silence," but always. God bless you, love, Pat.

On Thankfulness

I asked God for strength that I might achieve.
I was made weak that I might learn to obey.
I asked for health that I might do greater things.
I was given infirmity that I might do better things.
I asked for riches that I might be happy.
I was given poverty that I might be wise.
I asked for power that I might have the praise of men.
I was given weakness that I might feel the need for God.
I asked for all things that I might enjoy life.
I was given life that I might enjoy all things.
I got nothing that I asked for, but everything I had hoped for.
Almost despite myself, my unspoken prayers were answered.
I am, among all men, most richly blessed.
Thank You, God!

Sherry S. Cottingham
Indian Trail, NC

The Road Is My Own

The road is my own,
The path is one I choose.
With so many obstacles around me,
There is no time to lose.
My journey's just beginning,
As I grow older, each new day
Is filled with endless possibility—
Faith is lighting the way.
Walking down this single road,
I sometimes feel alone,
But if ever I lose my way,
I know help's waiting for me at home.
Though sometimes life is misguided,
Often seeming off-track,
Friends and loved ones wait to greet me
When I finally find my way back.
This road is not a smooth one,
It's sometimes rocky and overgrown,
But wherever life may take me,
I know the road is my own.

Melanie L. Morgan
Eagle, ID

Life

Life can be beautiful.
Life can be cruel.
Life's an adventure for genius or fool.
Some strive for perfection,
Some only get by,
Some have a vision, others only the eye.
It depends on perspective,
Whether to climb or to slide,
But whatever your choice, it's a spectacular ride.

Daniel Schears
Henderson, NV

How Will We Know?

How will we know when
It's really spring?
We'll know when the birds
Come back and sing.
When the skies are brightening
And the sun is enlightening
When the Earth is awakening
And beautiful buds are opening
When everything is blossoming
Then we'll know that
it's really spring!

Elinor Geiger
Flushing, NY

What Shall I Remember?

What shall I remember never to forget of the atrocious crime,
And Man's inhumanity to Man in God Almighty's name?

Will I see flailing bodies jumping through windows
High up from exploding towers, plummeting to eternity,
While collapsing buildings crush people helping people?

Will I feel the pain of charred and peeling flesh
Clinging to consoling hands only to be bathed away
By never-ending tears shed for those loved ones lost forever?

Will I sense the anguish and anxiety, the impatient wait
To know who lived or died,
Or the profound sorrow turning anger to hate
Toward those who chose this path of religious evil?

Is this a test by God of my compassion
And ability to forgive?

Patrick M. Growney
Villanova, PA

A True Friend

When in time of trouble and pain,
a true friend is one that's always there.
It is very easy to say I'm your friend,
but as I say, a true friend is one
that's always there.
A true friend is one that is always there.
When you are down and out in the cold,
and have no one to turn to, or have nowhere to go,
just pick up the phone and call your friend,
and no matter what, that friend will be there.
Amalia!
A friend in need is a friend indeed.
True friends like you are like a precious gem, hard to find.
When God made you, He made a one of a kind.
In you I've found a precious gem for a friend.
A true friend like you is very, very hard to find.
May God bless you always, my true friend.

Lisa Ann M. Gillings
Bronx, NY

The people in my life that inspired me are my kids, Tiyana, Jordan, Jamal, Jeanelle, and James, and my boyfriend, Elliot. My inspiration for writing poems is based on my life and things that happen in my life.

June Is Here!

Crackly little June bugs on the doorstep,
A stately robin hippity-hops.
A rainbow dancing in the sky,
Children chasing butterflies.
A beagle barking in his pen.
It's time to go a-hunting again.
The bees are humming, flowers in bloom
Mom's sweeping June bugs with her broom.
Apple pies are on the sill,
A weeping willow on the hill.
A bright red truck comes down the lane,
Bringing watermelon once again.
A rooster crowing loud and clear,
Chickens scurry far and near.
A toad is sitting in the dust,
Just watching all the flurry,
He sits so still, he's in no hurry.
A mother goose comes waddling by,
Her goslings march behind her.
Quacking and honking, keeping in step,
So perky, prim, and proper.
Yes, June is such a special month
When God has surely blessed.
As Pastor Tom has often said,
"Don't worry about the rest!"

Peggy H. Coffman
McKeesport, PA

Childhood memories inspired me to write this poem. My sister Janie and I were young and healthy farm girls enjoying our vacation in June of 1951. We remember Mom sweeping June bugs, Dad and his red truck, and the neighbor's beagles. We found little toads under our apple tree where Dad had made a swing for us out of bull rope and a piece of wood. The little farm animals gathered around us while Janie and I ate watermelon to our heart's content!

The Girl

She sits without being seen
Her five senses are so keen
She knows she doesn't belong
But she's done nothing wrong
She doesn't fit in
Not even with her kin
The pain in her heart
Is sharp as a dart
She's not like you
She's unique in all that she can do
She's really smart
And has much wisdom in her heart
She is a young girl
And has thoughts that twirl
So who is she?
Why . . . she is none other than me

Christina M. Morgan
Lavergne, TN

Of My Heart

Sleep doesn't come easy;
his eyes filling my dreams,
his voice suffusing my mind
to where I dare not stir,
lest I miss a single word that
falls from his lips.
He moves to enchant me, I know,
and that smile of Eire is
reason enough for breathing!
Would love dare introduce us
one to the other?
Our blood is ancient, yet
how evocative is this
sudden stirring of my heart!

Roxanna Caughey
Nashville, TN

Had it not been for my mom, my poetry would never have been seen. She saw a small contest advertisement in a magazine and showed it to me. I entered and received honorable mention. She was my biggest fan when she was alive. This poem was in my head when I awoke early one morning from a dream. Maybe that sounds corny, but yes, a dream inspired this poem. I've been writing, mostly poetry, since I was a teenager and though those days have passed, I still enjoy writing.

Seasons of My Life

You entered my life when I was
A lonely nineteen.
Suddenly, the days became joyful and
The sun shone warm, like a beam.

I woke each morning with a smile
I could not hide.
I skipped and danced,
A happy step was added to my stride

Many seasons have passed, and
I now am old.
You were taken from me
On a day that was so cold.

My thoughts journey back to
So many wondrous years.
I smile, I cry, I give thanks . . .
Still mixed with many tears.

Attea M. Barnes
Sterling Heights, MI

Come October

Come October, the winds will ease
As beautiful colors fall from the trees
Colors in brown, red, green, and gold
A beautiful sight for the eyes to behold

Come October, the air will be crisp and cool
As the little children toddle off to school
As summer comes to an end
A beautiful fall begins

Come October, the night is full of stars
As far as the eyes can see
As an old hoot owl sits high in a tree
The big golden moon starts to fade away
Hence the beginning of a new harvest day

Come October, there are carnivals all around
And ghosts and goblins all over town
The children have lollipops dancing in their heads
As they scurry home being late for bed

Shirley F. Woodruff
Sunray, TX

Lamentation

Boisterous chatter ceases silently
Warm breath coldly stills
Vacant eyes stare unseeing
Cherished years of life
So vibrant and uplifting
Now only pleasant remembrances
A decision made in love
Renders unending heartache

Heath A. Hoch
Ripon, WI

Softly

He comes to me softly
And bids me no fear.
He calls me to serve Him,
To feel His love near.
In His service of love
To my own fellowman,
My God bids me, come
With a touch of His hand.
My spirit shall soar
In the glory of all
Of His goodness and mercy.
I will answer His call.

Ernest N. Mills III
Jacksonville, TX

My Own Angel

I was sitting in my blue chair
Cancer I have, it's just not fair
An angel appeared so radiantly bright
My eyes blurred from all of the light
She spoke in a voice so calm, so real
I knew she surely was the real deal
Heaven also thinks cancer is unfair
Jesus sent me to show He does care
I've been here since you knelt to pray
Sins forgiven, remember, I'm here to stay
You won't see me again, but be not in fear
No matter what, I will always be near
I was sent to tell you of Heaven so high
As she spoke of Heaven, yes, I did cry
I looked around and my angel wasn't there
Was it a dream? Mind raced as I sat in my chair
Soon remission from cancer, so very true
Was it my angel? Jesus? Judge must be you

David V. Larson
St. Petersburg, FL

An Ode to My Alma Mater and to Haiti

"Why me?" is the unanswerable question
Why have I been picked to carry this unbearable burden?
The anguish, the grief, the tears running down a mom's face
The crouched shoulders, the helpless suffering,
A dad's forlorn look staring into space
And yet I see the strength, the determination,
The singular perseverance
That only comes from being a parent
Their fervent pleas of help send shivers down my spine
As their hearts for their missing children ache and pine
I ask, could I bear loss of such magnitude?
If the Fates dealt me the same cards,
Would I have the same fortitude?
Bring closure for all of Haiti, I do pray
May there be a silver lining among rubble-ridden clouds so gray
I hear encouraging voices of comfort and compassion
From those far and near
But only the ones left behind to suffer, wait, and fear
Seven days of uncertainty can take its toll
And still they steadfastly wait
A miracle perhaps shall bring back the ones they adore,
Their love and hope will not abate.

Hovi B. Shroff
Boca Raton, FL

God's House

Jesus is my Lord and King
To Him I raise my voice and sing
To sing of His wondrous work and love
And introduce someone to Him above

You needn't be afraid and full of awe
When you come to His house to pray
You don't have to impress anyone at all
Because God always hears what you will say

His house is full of joy and love
God sends it down from Heaven above
His people benefit from all this joy and love
So to someone else share God's love from above

So to God I raise my voice and sing
In hopes that someone will hear my song
And come to God's house and sing and sing
Because at God's house you can't go wrong

Dorothy J. West
Oklee, MN

Silly Sally

Silly Sally sat slightly sideways on
Simon's slippery slim slider.

Soon silly Sally slid slightly slowly sideways
down Simon's slippery slim slider.

Splat! sat silly Sally who slid slightly slowly
sideways on Simon's slippery slim slider.

So sad silly Sally sat sitting in slightly slimy sand
from sliding slightly slowly sideways on
Simon's slippery slim slider.

Sherrie L. Johnson
Phillipsburg, NJ

It's an honor to say I'm a spiritual person who puts God first. I'm a loving, supportive mom, daughter, and friend whose passions include loving and caring for my animals, writing, poetry, charities, volunteering, and art. If not for the unbelievable and outstanding support of my two daughters, who are the core of my soul, the reason my heart beats strongly every day, and who are truly the ones behind all the inspiration and success of all my writings. I'm forever blessed and thankful for Elizabeth and Crystal Johnson. Mom loves you!

The Disappearing Line

Words are spoken with promises being broken.
So the battle begins.
A line gets drawn. All thinking grows dim,
but still hope remains strong.
Eyes stare, piercing one's soul.
Feelings and emotions start taking their toll.
Time grows short and yet it seems long.
Soon a standstill is growing strong.

What to do? Everyone knows,
but how to do it is yet to be told.
The silence is deafening, so friends unite,
waiting and watching for the big fight,
but the fight never happens as the evading goes on,
and help from above is coming on strong.
Raindrops start falling and the wind starts to blow.
Now each side grows weary and both want to go.
So eventually they walk toward each other with arms open wide,
indicating the fading motion of the disappearing line.

Each side is able to keep their pride
and all because each one had forgiveness inside.

Esther M. Mogis
Holt, MI

When the lines that are drawn fail to disappear and are still left standing, we have
the Alamo and the Arlington Cemetery to think about. Also, too many lines are
being drawn, whether it's between different countries, family members, politicians,
or friends over little issues, even some that are forgotten and now seem unimportant.
These issues were never really brought to a conclusion and were just swept under
the rug, so to speak, keeping the ill feelings alive between these persons. I just want
all these ill feelings to disappear so happiness can flourish between them.

Just Being

Standing in the sand,
small waves wash
over my feet.

I can feel the sun rising
over my shoulder, a
warm breeze on my neck.

Gulls flying overhead,
calling to each other
at morning's fresh breath.

The mist, cool and crisp,
rests on my skin
and gleams with every move.

Contentment, release, and
comfort, I cannot help
but feel.

I am alive, mesmerized by
nature's beauty,
wrapped in her loving arms.

Joann C. Martinez
Concord, CA

Beara Peninsula

And it was there,
Embraced in rolling arms of infinite earth,
I discovered you,
Not for the first time, but for the finest time.
Though words were exchanged, none were needed.
We existed in worlds that were not our own.
As life buzzed around us, beneath us, with us,
Time rested beside us on those compassionate stones,
Along that placid lake,
In the lap of nature's best kept secret.
In the land where poetry is etched
In the rigid lines of mountainous grace,
On the teetering stones that enticed waves
Through liquid tranquility,
And imprinted on every contemplation
That sailed along the whispering winds,
We became stanzas in a poem a million years in the making.
And as misting Irish skies cleansed breath and sight and soul,
I wander through the shades of amber in your eyes.
And though the majesty of all the
Earth's treasures were laid at our feet,
It was the subtle beauty of your soul that captivates my mind still.
You
And me
And a moment
That would inspire a thousand wondrous memories;
Memories that have found a home on that rock, upon that lake,
In the lap of nature's best kept secret.

Julie E. Petrie
Pompton Lakes, NJ

A Journey's Blessing

The rose's yellow petals are for richness of the heart.
The leaves so green are for the richness of the soul.
The thorns of the rose are for the heartache we endure,
And the stem of the rose is the ladder we must climb
To reach the yellow petals of the rose.

Jessica L. Claycomb
Bedford, PA

The Lily and the Candle

The lily and the candle
Resting upon the table
A solitary form
Stately in appearance
Fragile with underlying strength
The white of innocence
Highlighted by the glow
A candle in the dark
To bring warmth to grow
Together there is life
No hope apart
The lily and the candle
May the candle forever cast its glow

Florence T. Compher
Hammonton, NJ

135

My Marine

Where's my marine, I wonder, he said,
In a country far away, a land not his own,
His heart so saddened, his feelings turned to dread,
A father thinking of his son who's far from home.

His reasons for going,
To make the old man proud,
Not already knowing
It was on the old man's brow.

The boy, now a man, was tall and straight,
A knight's heart he held in his breast.
He'd fought at the threshold of hell's gate,
He'd proven that courage was at his behest.

You're my hero, the old man told his son,
His proud old eyes beginning to tear.
In his heart he wished the war were won,
So all families would not have to fear.

Where's my marine?
He's wandering far from home.

Edmond T. Caouette
Corinth, VT

The Dream Slipped Away

It was the home I've dreamt of many years.
You'd think it was built for me.
Now all that's left are memories and tears.
I thought it was meant to be.
God placed my dream home at my door.
Opportunity knocked, but is there no more.
My money lay dormant in another house.
My hands were tied, the dream was lost that day.
Like quicksilver, it slipped away.
I believed I would buy it.
No, I'm not kidding.
I trusted someone else to do my bidding.
Twelve round columns, thirty inches around,
A pond and almost ten acres of ground.
Large round columns and open spaces
There was room to entertain happy faces.
God gave us a mind and the right to choose.
Our decisions decide if we win or lose.
Round columns, open spaces, and rooms were plenty
Room for a table to seat twenty,
Room for sharing, loving, giving, and living.
God blessed me with a chance to live my dream,
But I trusted someone else to do my bidding.
The dream slipped away with part of me that day.

Lawanda G. Gray
Pinville, LA

Throbbing Drums

Floating in the darkness,
blocking out all sounds,
sleep is overwhelming
until some pain abounds.
A throbbing, strong sensation
set within my hands
awakens me each morning
with some pounding rubber bands.
They constrict the joints and muscles
and make my tendons tight,
so inside each wrist and finger
strongly pain puts up a fight.
The tips of fingers well-used
get a mixture of these two,
they're numbness and pain on and off
with tingling through and through.
In order to remove the pain
and numbness that I feel,
an operation must be done,
replenishing life's zeal.
Hopefully that action
will take away their reign,
removing all the numbness
and replacing all the pain.
So then I'll sleep so soundly
until the sunlight comes
and get eight hours deeply
without the throbbing drums.

Deborah K. Parker
Central Islip, NY

I am a brain-injured adult that caught encephalitis at the age of fifteen by a mosquito that was carrying the virus. My cognitive problems and my memory impairment are all injuries from the virus. It gave me a seizure disorder. My interest in poetry was brought on by my mother, who was an English teacher throughout most of my childhood, and she wrote poetry herself. She taught me how to create words that flow with a rhythm and a rhyme coming from my heart. This poem is about the carpal tunnel surgery I had done on my right hand in 2006.

Sea Journey

Love is like a sailing ship
Abounding on the main,
Enjoyed both the sunshine
And the driving rain.
When you embark upon the sea
Of married life and bliss,
Sometimes the waters calm,
Sometimes they snarl and hiss.
The beauty of the seasons,
Romantic is the moon,
The birds, the flowers, the animals,
A drifting brown sand dune.
All the good things of nature
Are put here just for you,
And life tilts toward the positive,
This fact I know is true.
So if the captain and the crew
Maintain a steady course,
Keep an eye upon a star
And know that God's the source
Of hope and strength and happiness.
These traits will show the way
To a love that's great and meaningful
That will grow from day to day.

William C. Bard
Lancaster, PA

Dilemma 2010

There was a time in days gone by
when people were quite reasonable
and politicians disagreed
without being disagreeable.

They had their special preferences
but still, usually they could
put aside their differences
for the country's common good.

The world has had its special moments
and successes that were great
but now I can't remember when
it was filled with so much hate.

Some mean-spirited individuals
join a hostile band of brothers.
Some will sacrifice their life
to destroy the life of others.

We all have to work together
in our many varied lives
if we hope to have a future
where democracy survives.

Helene H. Nixon
Oakland, CA

I write verse for fun and especially enjoy telling a story in rhyme. I think it is an interesting form of narration that can be challenging for the writer and entertaining for the reader. Eagle Lake, Texas is where I was born on March 2, 1910. When I was four years old, we moved to Minnesota. My family owned a summer resort in northern Minnesota near Park Rapids. My college major was early childhood education. I had teaching experiences in Minnesota, Arizona, and California, and was the early education consultant for the Stockton, California Unified School District for many years.

Easton Dam

It was during my high school days
that our family bought a large chunk
of property in Easton Township in
Central Wisconsin.

As a recent Eagle Scout, I quickly
ventured into the woods, compass in hand.
Whoa! In no time, I reached a small stream,
flowing east to west.

Donning hip boots, I ventured up stream,
and was I surprised at all the springs
oozing water down the sides
that increased the flow of the stream.

This stream, called Campbell Creek,
gathers more water as it winds through
properties and under roads, wending its way
southwest to Lake Wisconsin.

For decades, a dam under a road, backed the
creek up to form Easton Lake. When the dam
erodes away, the dam and road were removed.

Wisconsin and Adams County agreed to
finance a new Easton Dam. Cofferdams
redirected the creek around the workers.

Now the inlet control structure and culvert are
completed, with Campbell creek rushing
through the new dam. Next is to refill the lake,
rebuild the road, and stock the lake with fish.

David L. Kennedy
Adams, WI

I was a technical writer most of my life. I graduated from University of Wisconsin, Stout in 1965. I retired fifteen years ago and moved into the country in Adams County, Wisconsin. Now I write stories and captions for my digital photos that are published in our weekly newspaper. When I learned that the state of Wisconsin and Adams County would fund the rebuilding of Easton Dam, I took photos of what once was Easton Lake—reduced to an area of green growth, with Campbell Creek meandering through it. I have been having photos published to show its progress.

Soldier

Hold on.
He tells her not to let go.
He would leave her that day
When he had just become hers.
She was afraid of losing the one person that meant most.
To the place that she dreaded most.
It's what he yearned to do,
To leave, to fight.
She would always love him.
That's what scared her most.
What if he left her
Alone in the cold, harsh storm
Where she wouldn't know how to deal?
The lasting kiss that meant goodbye pierced her lips.
It burned her mouth.
A lasting tear rolled heavily down her cheek,
Maybe forever.
A soldier for her.
A soldier for the world.

Meghan S. Groves
Divide, CO

The Lady of Grandeur

She isn't as long as she is deep
She isn't as wide as she is steep
From morning to night, her colors change
From a dapper grey to a great wide range
Of orange, reds, and shady hues
With shadows that many climbers user
She houses deer and antelope, and strangers
Many hikers walk through her forest
And on trails, facing many dangers
Of jagged rocks and great dehydration
If they don't watch for a water station
She is in northern Arizona with both
North and South Rims
Has snow in the winter, her own trim
She's a canyon to be admired
With her beauty and style
Please remember she is grand
And has been around for a while
The Grand Canyon is her name
And the Colorado River lends to her fame

Linda J. Hendrick
Jonestown, PA

I write from experience. I lived and worked in the Grand Canyon for four months.
I am married with three children and three stepchildren. We have a total of ten
grandchildren. We live in Lebanon, Pennsylvania. I am a disabled veteran, which
gives me plenty of time to write about life's journey.

Voices of Life's Sound

Sharing and giving, loving and dreaming
is all that makes the world go around.
Cries and laughter, whispers and shouting,
the wonderful voices of life's sound.

Opening one's mind for a deeper understanding
of what makes another react.
Narrow minded thinking only builds walls,
the bricks are already stacked.

Time to demolish all that is negative
to clear a path for us to see.
Varied are our duties and the roadways
to reach our destiny.

Our strength within must be released
to stand our common ground.
If you wish to hear cries and laughter, whispers and shouting
of the wonderful voices of life's sound!

Ozzie G. Davis
Troy, OH

To My Love

When first I saw you, it was the third of July,
You were quite busy and flying high.
So much to see and so much to do,
You didn't notice me, but I sure noticed you.

Sporting good looks with charisma that would not quit,
I couldn't help watching you, not for one bit.
I wanted to meet you so badly, it hurt,
But you were not interested, you wouldn't flirt.

As fate would have it, I became close friends with your mom,
We hung out, had good times, and we seemed to really get on.
It wasn't long before we were living together.
We were very close, just like birds of a feather.

The years that followed were simply the best,
Having you in my life made me feel truly blessed.
We had good times working or playing around,
We had quiet times with just us not making a sound.

A horrible day just recently hit us like a rock,
It happened after a routine trip to the doc.
They told us you were sick—actually, really ill,
As I ponder the news, I can't believe it still.

They say you won't be with me for a much longer time,
But I look into your eyes and your love still shines.
No matter what I will stay with you until the end,
You mean a lot to me, more than just a dear friend.

More than a dear friend is to state it lightly,
All I want to do is hold on and hug you tightly
Because you are one of the best puppies I ever knew,
For now and for always, Chief, I love you!

LuAnne R. Pugh
Pittsburg, KS

Delusions

Spacey thoughts . . . can they scare me?
Whispers nowhere coming from.
Voices shouting now and visions
From eyes closed
Do haunt me moments long.

Spacey thoughts don't scare me,
They come at half-past three.
Loud silence ceases
With hum of fridge,
And voices calling me.

Spacey thoughts don't scare me.
I've conquered them before.
Blinders now
Go 'round my head,
Illusions fall to floor.

Spacey thoughts don't scare me,
I have them all the time.
Though moments lost,
Years—decades, too;
Still to sky, my soul will climb.

Annette J. Teixeira
Oroville, CA

Sweet Baby Boy

You traveled so far to be born.
Your birthplace? A stable so forlorn.
What did your earthly Father, Joseph, do
while Mary was giving birth to You?
Did he wait outside and back and forth pace,
or did he help You emerge Your face?
And Mary, how did she fare?
Were her labor pains very hard to bear?
It is obvious, at least to me,
that Mary and Joseph were not ready
for Your arrival, sweet baby.
A small shawl was not even among the things
they had brought with which to enwrap a King.
Ah, but God was well prepared, you see,
for this was precisely the time and place
to herald His heavenly baby.
Fanfare and frivolity were never meant to be
the way You would serve humanity.
Therefore, the birthing of You, immaculate child,
was completed at just the right time
in just the right style.
Oh, sweet baby boy, whom I adore,
You were born so that mortals,
even as wretched as I,
might live forevermore.

Jeri D. Walker-Boone
Laurens, SC

I am a retired state of South Carolina employee. My poetry writing began when I was in my teens. Most of the poems I have penned have been for family and friends. God is the inspiration for all of my poetry and the majority of my poems are geared toward religious ideas. I have a catch phrase, which I adopted for my readers. "If you like the poem, then it is the result of God's inspiration. If the poem is a failure, then it the result of my perspiration."

Untitled

1996/2007

It seemed a snowflake in a flower pod;
snapping its revealing color of whitish purple,
then it dissolved as Styrofoam would.
There are several—lots—individually wrapped in
white coats of flakes like violets;
they were made, born out of nature's July warmth
on a mountainous hill, and lingering on the clayish brown soil
on this summer's day.

Michele M. Mena
Sanford, FL

Come and Go

People come
People go
Treasures come
Treasures go
We learn, some knowledge stays with us
While some we lose sight of
Yet you, my dear, you may stay
Or you may leave
Yet our souls will live together forever
Because I love you

Phyllis M. Nebus Volk
Aberdeen, NJ

To My Hubby

To celebrate our beautiful day
there are a few things I want to say
Of our forty-five years of bliss
there's nothing I'd want to miss

We've had a beautiful life together
Of course, as life goes, we've had some storms to weather
but when I look through the memories of a book
it is the good memories I choose to look

We've traveled over the beautiful USA
of all fifty states I'm proud to say
There is no better country I'd like to see
or with anyone my companion to be

Always remember I love you
to you I'll always be true
for with our hearts combined as one
we're still in for a lot of fun!

Carol Kemnitz
Palmdale, CA

Haiku in Spring

Cattle in meadow
Sniff eat and swallow each leaf
Evening cowbell rings.

Spring sunshine reaches
Out for miles and miles about
Earthworm settles down.

In nests among trees
Speckled eggs await the rise
Of pecking inside.

Breaking branches wind
Humming of thunder no bird
Songs spells midwest storm.

Green fields and clover
Smelling crops brought children to
Play in hills of hay.

Small birds sleep high in
Trees so cats and such are not
As free to disturb.

Ramona Kruse
Rochester, MN

Gems

Could a father find a jewel so rare
As his loving daughter's heart?
Could precious gems give the radiance
His daughter's smile imparts?

He might search the wide world over
And the void of outer space,
But never match the brilliant glow
Of his daughter's smiling face.

Rare diamonds brightly sparkle
Like the stars in yonder skies,
But nothing sparkles half so much
As a loving daughter's eyes.

His daughter's love, a treasure trove
Of wealth and joy combined,
More precious than the finest gold
That has ever been refined.

It's a wealthy father to be sure
Who has a loving daughter,
And richer still, if he's so blessed
As to hold his own granddaughter!

Roger H. Arnett
Rochester, MN

151

Give Love, Get Love

To live our life on through day to day
Within the perils and our happy time,
With all the things that will come our way,
Sometimes it seems to blow our minds.

Step back and make a strong effort
To stay on the straight and narrow road
That leads the way right from the heart
And soul so we can carry the load.

All you have to do is stay with the Lord,
And God will keep you in His grace.
Then you can keep up with God's Word,
And handle anything that you may face.

Then the love of God will be with you
In all your days that you may live,
So keep the faith in all you go through.
We will be judged on the love that we give.

Harry E. Dearen
Houston, TX

Night and Moon

The other night, I walked out front with my son.
He was going to his home. When he was leaving,
The moon was full and looked not too far away.
It was a beautiful evening,
But of course,I knew it was miles and miles away
Even though it looked large and full.
I knew it was there and would be there to stay.
I could almost see a smiling face looking at me,
And all the wonder of God was there for us to see.
I have lost so may of my family and friends
And things that I really loved.
No one knows how much I have been hurt,
No one but God above.
I have been really lonely and it hurts,
And things are not right, but I try not to complain
And just go on with my life.
The world is getting to be out of hand
And hard at times, but we have to do our best.
I hope and pray I have done or said something
To my family and friends so they will remember me.
I hope I'll go to see God and my loved ones
Will be there and with God's help, I'll try my best.

Dorothy M. Walters
Dresden, TN

I have had a hard life in a lot of ways. I lost my husband, mother, father, sister,
brother, and granddaughter. I started writing poetry from the loneliness, I guess. I
am eighty-two years old and I live alone. I enjoy writing. Please pray for me, even
though you don't know me; we are all God's children.

Searching for Sanity

I am trying to find a good mind,
a will that is free; one
not merely rambling,
but a will first-rate,
that combined, these could anticipate
more rational ways and means.

I am searching for peace,
peace that will last, peace
that might cast
some warm sunlight on a darkened past.

I've searched long and hard,
(my foolishness showing)
never really knowing
when the pain would stop.
For the good of my future,
some hope I'll save,
but I may never be sane
till I'm down in my grave.

David T. Panagotis
Poughkeepsie, NY

Another Room

I've heard the sounds
of penury.
It's rising liturgy
through the night.
Bulb-eye open
through the night
comprehends the plight . . .
from the land
of penury.

Cynthia J. Tinckler
Ocean Grove, NJ

Spring Is Glowing

Spring is glowing
Wildflowers growing

Robins singing
Joys of spring ringing

Songs whispered through trees
Carried by the breeze

Warm spirits of spring
Bring out the best in everything

Debra L. Phillips
Tumwater, WA

Take Time to Smell the Flowers

"Have you ever heard the old saying,
take time to smell the flower?"
It works like this:
Give what you have to others,
be it little or much.
If you can't write a book,
You can still keep in touch.
"Who is out there eager to hear
from a friend?"
You can send a message of Cheer.
If you'll not elected to Congress,
No doubt you can smile.
Perhaps make someone's life worth while.
Take the time to smell the flowers.
The things you thought you couldn't do,
Just remember this:
God made you for a special assignment-
That you alone can do.

Connie Holt
Waynesboro, TN

Writing poetry has always been my passion. Creative memories of a way to express myself, a good way how I feel about family and friends. "Take Time to Smell the Flowers" is about taking a long hard look on what is happening around us, what others are doing, and how they see things. If they need help in any way, it doesn't take much to give your time to someone in need. But it sure adds up big in kindness. Try it. You'll like it. All of it is a good antidote for a runaway kind heart.

Pacific Universe

Once upon a summer night
the sea was full of stars,
little sparkling galaxies
that danced and swirled for hours.

Passing fish left comet trails
that took my breath away.
Although midnight had come and gone,
I wanted still to stay.

Tiny creatures were pin-sized lights
in the darkness of the deep.
While they hurried on their way,
I would not yield to sleep.

Who could turn away from all
the beauty swimming by?
Who could not be mesmerized?
Certainly not I.

I have no clue to the source
of this glory, no cold scientific reply.
All I have is a sense of awe
at the magic passing by.

I'm caught by the wonder, the mystery.
What makes these sea creatures glow?
As I lie on the dock to trace their paths,
I realize I may never know.

Sherry A. Preston
Craig, AK

Never a Good Day

Just like the rumble of thunder
Splitting the sky apart with lighting,
A iron tank, spitting fire, explodes a shack
Into a thousand pieces. Its splintered
Parts rain down on the barren desert like
A gentle rain on a field of red clover, but it is not
A field of red clover. It is a blood-red field of war.
Before it's over, a cloud of stinking black smoke
Will cover the ravaged country. Thousands of people
Will be killed or maimed. Men. Women. Children. Rich.
Poor. It matters not. Dead is dead.

I stand gazing at the useless ruins of war.
Thinking, how can this be?
How and why does this happen
To those, to you, to me?

I bow my head. I turn and walk away.
A salty tear drops from my eye.
Tucking my hands beneath my arms, I say,
"There is never a good day to die."

Michael M. Cain
Meadville, MS

Castaway (The Defiant One)

Cast adrift on the sea of life
far away from the shore
Between the darkness and the light
with the rain coming down
just what the future has in store
I don't know but I'll fight for
the right to be the best I can

Just like a soldier on the run
here with no place to hide
From the war that rages deep inside
a war I'll fight till I die
I'll have my moment in the sun
but just when I'm not certain
this rain keeps pouring down on me

Against the tide and the raging sea
of one thing I am certain
The will to forge our destiny
is a fire still burning
Of just one thing we're in command
it's a part of the master plan
the choice of sides on which to stand

Bruce M. Ajamian
Little Egg Harbor, NJ

No Spigot

The moments of day run rushing like a stream filled with snow runoffs,
waiting for the whispering wind from your lips to slow the rush.

The short pause your lips offer to the rushing energy is spirit-filled,
flooding the banks of my heart to anew shoreline.

The floods of my heart falsely resemble lust with love at the core,
pumping heat waves into the snow banks
till avalanches fall into the stream.

Cheryl A. Wineinger
West Palm Beach, FL

I have been writing poems since I was in the fourth grade and received my first blue
ribbon at the Tennessee Valley Fair. Currently, I have entered the world of children's
books. I have four books completed, including the pictures I painted for them. The
books are just awaiting the proper publishing company. This poem was a result of a
special relationship. Relationships are the most natural and meaningful interaction
in life; therefore, I selected a natural process to depict this relationship. Once the
relationship and the process is started, there's no ending, thus no spigot to turn off.

A Poem of Praise

I thank God for this special life.
I know I am like no other.
Feeling and seeing and giving love
As a wife and supporting mother.
I'm enjoying life's beauties,
The flowers of all colors,
The night skies on fire, with colors untold
The cream-colored yellows and purples and gold.
The night stars shining
On white-capped waving waters,
The moon slowly rising
Sometimes full, sometimes just quarters.
The wonder is touching,
The song of life rarely heard,
Except for early morning
In the sweet song of a bird!

Ruthanne Lyons
Margate, FL

I have been working along with my first novel. Almost completed, I find myself escaping into a field very unusual from my all-encompassing characters. Poetry— the words come gently from the pen and find their space on my paper. My spirit is stretching and taking a sudden change. This is one of life's pleasures when you are a writer; I am enjoying the moment!

First

When her eyes first opened on this world,
the first thing she would see,
dark olive brown, an infant's crown,
she focused first on me.

When her laugh first burst a quiet room,
her noise of joy or tears,
I was there where Mother's loom
first heard her with these ears.

When first she took those little steps
not yet a yardstick tall,
it was I with eagle eye who reached
to break her fall.

The first arms that would hold her tight
that felt her soft design,
of all those arms she'd find at night,
her first embrace was mine.

Of all those lips she burned and quit
and things she could not speak,
her first kiss she could not forget
I put upon her cheek.

Those countless ones she loved untrue
and blew away like smoke,
no, none could love her like I do,
my heart, the first she broke.

Kimmerle S. Ramos
Elmont, NY

What God Has for You, It Is for You

What God has for you, it is for you.
What God has for you, it is for you!
In spite of all you may go through,
what God has for you, it is for you!
Heartaches and disappointments,
what God has for you, it is for you!
Setbacks and lacking what you need,
what God has for you, it is for you!
Lack of support, encouragement, and confidence from others
as you strive to make it the best you can,
what God has for you, it is for you!
Struggles with health, spiritual/religious, finances, family, academics,
goals, dreams,
martial, career, job-related issues, etc.,
what God has for you, it is for you!
When Satan tries to have a stronghold on your life
by doing all he can to tear you down,
by what others may say and do,
keep in mind, you are a child of a loving God
who's an all-merciful, powerful deliver, provider,
healer, restorer, etc.
So try to keep a mustard seed of faith,
believing with hope and determination that
what God has for you, it is for you!
And give Him praises!

Kimberly Best
East Orange, NJ

I am blessed. I thank God for inspiring me to use my heartfelt "Godspirational" poetry writing, hopefully to His glory and purpose. I share this particular poem in hopes it will be a blessing to all who read it and will be inspired, realizing whatever they are going through, still hold on to that mustard seed of faith in knowing what God has for you, it is for you!" I especially dedicate this poem to all my special kids, my mentor, friend, and national Blue Ribbon Award recipient, Linda Thompson, and other dear supportive friends and family.

No Friend

I try to tell them that you're no friend.
They say you are till the very end.
You consume their lives
and make them blue,
yet they keep coming back to you!
You are fun at the start,
then slowly convince them
that you should never be apart.
You push away their good sense
till they end up alone
on the other side of the fence.
Some learn you can't be trusted,
but only after they've been busted.
You go by many names,
some fact, some fiction,
so—
I'll just pen you as addiction!

Rose Knight
Bayshore, NY

Beloved

Where your restless spirit dwells
I'd like to be.
Far and near the mind does travel,
My soul is craving thee.

The dent is left where oft you sat,
I touch it with my hand
Imagining your body's warmth
Will stay there till time's end.

The mirror on the wall
Does it reflect your smile?
You coat so lonely hanging in the hall
Now for the longest while.

Your shoes waiting at the door
For feet that loved to walk.
I still hear footsteps on the floor,
So quietly they talk.

Will you return someday
The soul again at ease,
Or memories just float away
Like petals in a breeze?

Ursula M. Kandaris
New York, NY

I grew up surrounded by beautiful nature, forests and lakes in abundance, wild animals and tame ones to admire and play with. Nature has always been my inspiration and solace in trying times. Trained as a ballerina, I had to give up my dream career due to disabling back injuries. After a failed marriage and a business career, I'm finally retired and have time for all my creative hobbies.

A Senior Citizen Wish

The snow is falling all around
Freezing as it hits the ground.
The squirrels are running up and down.
Picking up the nuts that are on the ground.

The weather is hard on folks like me.
I am a senior citizen, you see.
We can't go out, you know,
So we stand and look out the door,
Praying for God's mercy to melt the snow.

Check on us if you please
To see if it's anything we need.
God bless you for looking after us,
It is His will,
Because God is love so it's a must
To look after folks like us.

Evelyn S. Clayborn
Saisbury, NC

My Prayer

God of the mighty universe,
the mountains and the sea,
what an awesome thought it is
to know You care for me.

God, who holds the sun and moon,
and all the stars in Your hand,
when my tiny world falls apart,
You help me understand.

God, who has the thunder and
lightning in Your control,
You're always there to help me,
and bring peace within my soul

God, who has forever been,
and will forever be,
someday, through faith,
I'll be in Your presence,
and Your face I'll see.

Lydia A. Smoak
Rock Hill, SC

On Top of Old Baldy

On top of Old Baldy,
No hair on our head,
We're going through chemo,
No more need be said.
I opted for full shave,
No fallout for me,
Became a true egghead,
As you plainly see.
Our beauty's from inside,
Don't look in the mirror,
Skin deep doesn't measure
Why we're really here.
A V stands for vic'try,
A sign that we share,
We're fighting a battle
That few others dare.
We don't need your pity,
We don't need your tears.
We do need you love,
Your support, and your cheer.

Elaine M. Uonelli
Perry, OH

I wrote my first poem, "Tajah," in 1989, after a car hit our toy poodle. Putting the sadness into words helped assuage some of the sorrow. Numerous writings followed inspired by experiences, special occasions, events, and unique people. "Fragments" is a self-published collection of my work. "On Top of Old Baldy" emerged during my bout with lymphoma and chemotherapy. I consider reading and writing poetry therapy for the soul. Expressing feelings, thoughts, and ideas and sharing them with others completes me. Joy follows when readers relate to a poem and reveal their own interpretations.

Pain

Heal my wound,
take the pain.
End this torture,
keep me sane.

The pain inside
is just too real.
Make me numb
so I can't feel.

Stop the voices,
silence them please.
I'm begging, pleading,
I'm on my knees.

Take the drama,
and the grief.
Give me silence,
and sweet relief.

Patricia A. Childress
Mooresboro, NC

To Sodom's Minions

Oh, Sodom's minions fall in haste
And chafe under the yoke divine
To ravish hot, the virgin chaste.

Survey the region's blighted waste
In hatred's passion low repine—
Oh, Sodom's minions fall in haste.

In Hell's dominion dark, embrace
Black Satan's gulf, his livid brine
To ravish hot, the virgin chaste.

As starry Heaven's fallen race
Seal on their heads the dreaded sign
Oh, Sodom's minions fall in haste.

Demonic hordes, in vile disgrace
To Styx by Satan's plot consign
To ravish hot, the virgin chaste.

Accursed, you fiery lot embrace
Beguiled by Satan's flawed design.
Oh, Sodom's minions fall in haste
To ravish hot, the virgin chaste.

Jay L. Lawson
Waco, TX

Flag Day

The word "flag" has many meanings
It all depends on its usage,
But there is one that gives a good gleaning,
That is Flag Day, thus is not abusive!

Many seem to forget its significance
That it had a great beginning
Many, many years ago in the USA,
And has remained without its ending!

It's a special marked day on our calendars
Whether it is noticed or not,
But it is to all our soldiers,
And all others should not let it be forgot!

So let us remember it without any spikes,
It was on June 14, 1777 without any fake
When Congress proclaimed the Stars and Stripes
The national standard of the United States of America!
Hallelujah!

Elizabeth C. Funk
White Salmon, WA

I was born in Portsmouth, Virginia, in December 1920. My husband, Chester L. Funk, was in the military; thus, we moved a lot. My deceased husband and parents, John and Emma Prosch, were always supportive of my writing. Some of my poems have been published and put on tape here in the U.S. and also overseas, which naturally pleases me. Writing poems gives me great pleasure. I thank you for asking me to send you one and am happy you are publishing it.

God's Beauty

I opened my curtain
This morning to view
A burst of beauty
In a grand debut.

A tree that opened
Its loveliness in the night
To welcome the morning
For my greatest delight.

Its trunk is gnarled
And crooked and old,
But the color of its foliage
Is a sight to behold.

As I gazed at the blossoms
In their exquisite prime,
I know He makes everything
Beautiful in its time.

Lael J. Nabhan
Hobart, IN

After

After today
There's tomorrow

After the calm
There is the sorrow

After the sad
There is the glad

After the yesterday
There is today

And tomorrow
Another day

Deanna L. Widowson
Columbus, OH

I started writing poetry about fifteen years ago. This particular poem I just thought up in mind one day. I like writing poems. I work at the Hyatt Regency Hotel, Columbus, Ohio, in the housekeeping department as a laundry attendant. I have two cats, Chance and Atlas. I have been married to my husband for nineteen years. I would love to be your grand prize winner.

Nature's Lips

The sun high above the grassy plains.
The trees cast shadows upon the land so long.
Flowers turned their faces toward the bright.
A slight breeze danced across the grasses' blades.
No soul doth challenge such a wondrous sight.
For today, silence will rule God's Earth at last.
Not a cloud above to ruin this delight.
The tenderness of leaves show change.
They fall with grace and frolic through the wind.
How can it be that such a day has come?
The smiling nature pleased with what she's done.
Whistles escape the wind as it blows by.
The footsteps of a nearby fawn are not enough to cause disturbance.
Birds fly by, a gleam in their eyes, pleased to spread their wings.

Lisa M. Hegedus
Westerville, OH

Trees

Bountiful, plentiful trees
Rise from ground roots
To skyward; tall, leafless,
Forming shiny coated bark
Hidden trunk
Beautifies park
As riveresque arms, branches
Melt unto tiny streams
Leaving breathable oxygen.

Debra A. Gauvin
Seymour, CT

Untitled

Holding my own broken heart
in my own hands, I wonder how
it will ever heal.

My heart still beats and slowly
pulls itself back together, only
to be pulled apart time after time.

I rage against the night like
an angry wolf and try to take
a bite out of the moon.

Kent R. Thornton
Council Bluffs, IA

Life's Profound Simplicity

It's not the rhythm you will feel,
Nor is it something that can heal.
It's not the gentle flow of sound
That leads your heart to where it's bound.

It's not the love of those who care,
Nor is it something some will share.
It's not the semblance of the verse,
Nor will it bring a tone of curse.

It's not the story you can tell,
Nor is it tales of life that sell.
It's not the woe of old and new
That helps us touch the morning dew.

It simply is a poem, you see,
Poetic as this poem can be.
It warms the heart and heals the soul,
Belonging to those who fit the mold.

Joyce M. Partise
Los Angeles, CA

I am a blessed woman who is approaching my eightieth birthday. Although I am an only child, I'm never lonely. I am widowed with two children, twins, a boy and a girl. I found myself writing this poem one day as I reflected upon my life, with its trials and tribulations. Life is really quite simple, I thought. We are born, we grow, we pray, while we wait to return home to the Lord.

Broken Love

I looked out my window,
watched the snow falling down.
It was early in the morning,
you took the train ride into town.
The words in your letter
said you wanted to be alone.
Now here I am with memories
of a new year's sad song.

It's useless to hold the tears back
as they slide down my face.
A day I'll spend without you,
guess the wine will take your place.
The sleep will overtake me,
a time of wasted day.
This sudden change you have of me
can't take this game you play.

Maybe by tomorrow,
you'll find another nest.
You always made the mention of
someone you knew out west.
But just remember one thing
so you will surely know,
don't come knockin' on my door,
'cause I may never show.

John D. Ball
Marion, VA

Old Glory

Old Glory is an apt nickname
for the flag of our republic.
It has stood the test of time,
and weathered every conflict.
From Bunker Hill and Annapolis,
from the masts of our ships at sea,
Old Glory still stands for freedom
for all the world to see.
The marines on Iwo Jima
raised the flag in victory,
a symbol of America's fight
against hate and tyranny.
Some folks desecrate the flag,
use fire to snuff it out;
these people don't have the slightest clue
what this country is all about.
America stands for freedom,
for the rights of all mankind.
She will fight until her final breath
so no one is left behind.
So let Old Glory's stars and stripes
unfurl throughout our land.
"Let freedom ring and peace prevail"
will ever be our stand.

Richard L. York
Thomasville, NC

In Loving Memory of Our Parents

The things you did helped to keep us straight
For this we dearly appreciate
You were only grooming us to do what was right
To walk by faith and not by sight
You taught us that we are the head and not the tail
To trust in Jesus He will never fail

Oftentimes we didn't understand
When you gave us strong demands
You encouraged us to hold on to God's unchanging hand
To serve only God and not Man
That we are above and not beneath
And all that we are we should bequeath

To walk with the Lord for He is our guide
Where peace and love abide
When we feel the need to give up
Take another sip from the Lord's cup
With your loving guidance and our hard labor
We are truly blessed and highly favored

Jearlene Sanders
Maysville, NC

I was born November 3, 1947 to the late Thomas and Florena Canady in Maysville, North Carolina. Children: Kellie Christopher and Nevalyn (Fefe). I graduated from Jones High School in Trenton, North Carolina, class of 1966. Career accomplishments: Nurse's assistant, Girl Scout leader, CDA certificate, Cuyahoya Community College Cleveland, Ohio. Certificate of cashier checker. I am a member of Saint Luke AME Zion Church in Maysville, North Carolina. Following capacities: Church secretary, president, gospel choir, senior choir, the ladies' and gents' auxiliary, class leader number four, President of WHOM Society, YES department, financial secretary for the Newbern District Lay Council. This poem is dedicated to the loving memory of our parents, Thomas W. Canady and Florena Bradley Canady.

Mother and I

My mother's tiny and petite
While I am large and not as neat.
She loves to eat just healthy meals
While I think fast foods are "a deal."
She exercises every day
While I keep finding time to stray.

She loves to sing and entertain,
I like to let the TV reign.
She's loved by everyone she meets,
While I appear not quite as sweet.
She's honest, faithful and sincere,
But my good traits do not appear.

Whatever differences we claim,
We love each other just the same.
Our births are twenty years apart
But that will never change our heart.
We'll stay as partners to the end
Because we are the best of friends.

Marlene R. Murrell
Calimesa, CA

I have been writing poetry since the 1960s for my own pleasure. The majority of my poetry is written for other people who seek me to write a poem covering a situation in their life that is important to them. I believe mine is a God-given talent for myself and the special people who, having need for inspirational support, somehow come into my life. This particular poem was written and presented to my sweet mother at her ninety-fifth birthday party. I am hoping to publish a manuscript to prove to the world that rhyming poems can be short stories.

Today a Pair of Black Swans Came for a Visit

It was a dreary, heartless gray day,
Spreading a heavy blanket of clouds upon us.
No luster of light to brighten tired blades of grass.
Then, droplets of rain splashed on the veranda railing.
They kept striking like the melancholy strings of a harp.

Lazy rivulets of water slid down with sharp footsteps
Upon the grass, the leaves, the green shawl of the trees.
Suddenly, a flock of swans surrounded my home,
White, gray, and black ones in splendid dresses
With proud long necks and their majestic dancing walk.
Pure, gracious beauty from the unexpected flock.
Nothing wild in their stance, nothing unfriendly,
Especially the black swans in their elegant tuxedos,
Reminded me of charming dancer Fred Astaire—dandy!

Then a pair of black swans left their flock
And came near me to sit close by my veranda railing.
The wing of a male was over his mate,
Sheltering her from a drizzling autumn rain.
She, in answer, spread her feathers, touching him,
Wishing for a silky nest of her tender lover's dream.

Surprisingly, the sky cast a glorious melody of light,
Chiseling God's blessing upon this pair of lovers
In a live, golden sculpture of eternal love.

Lubov L. Kolensky
Wayne, NJ

I enjoy writing immensely. Books were my first love—poetry is my passion. Poetry is like my twin sister—sometimes disappointing, other times, triumphant! "Through difficulties to the stars" is my motto. A lifetime writer and journalist, I majored in philosophy and English literature to earn a bachelor's degree at the University of Innsbruck, Austria. Later, I edited the Ukrainian-American newspaper *Svoboda* for over a decade. I was recently honored as a distinguished member of the Penn Club and The International Society of Poets. My poetry also appears in two earlier books, *The Best Poems and Poets*, 2006 and 2007.

Analogy

People are like raindrops.
Some stand firm
And hold their ground,
While others just dissipate
Into the universe.

They traverse my skin
Like fingertips,
The ones I long for
To caress me
Ever so gently.

Will you maintain
Your facade,
Or will you break down
And show me love
Like I know you feel?

Please be strong.
We will make it,
I promise.
We won't evaporate
Like the rain.

Abigail J. Pardue
Bemus Pt, NY

Old Friends

Old friends are quite a treasure
They're like a comfortable shoe
They'll always protect and support you
No matter what you do
They'll always stand beside you
They'll never let you down
That shoulder is always there
Even when you wear a frown
When everything is going wrong
Old friends are there to call
They won't turn away
When things get rough
They will never let you fall
When my life is over
And my journey in this world ends
I'll know it was worth the living
Because of my old friends

Randy A. Brown
Hamilton, IN

Thank You, Dad

I don't remember the last time
I said, "Thank you, Dad."
I have been busy as things go.
You were there for the first bike ride,
You helped me with my first car.
I just forgot.

You helped me with the college move.
I thought I had.
You paid for college,
I am a better person for that.
For the walks and the talks,
Thought I had for that, too.

So Dad, for being the man you are,
for being the father you have been
That's made me the man I am,
I thank you for that, Dad.

Francesca Echevarria
Milford, PA

Sharing Love

The world we live in is so sad.
We really should cherish the things we have.
If people would share their love and compassion,
The world would be a better place to live in.

There's so much beauty all around us to share.
God gives us His blessings, His love, and His care,
Such as miracles to see, touch, and hear.
We need to focus on the needs of others,
For only through sorrow, God gives us refuge.
But God reminds us that one can give without loving,
But never can one truly love without giving.

Our loving God, who is our Creator,
He teaches us to love one another.
So be glad for God's blessings, His love, and His care.
Bless everyone who walks with love,
They also walk with our God above.

Joyce G. Wentovich
Wyalusing, PA

The Price of Freedom

Innocent faces, unknown places,
fighting to survive, trying to stay alive.
Through a haze of dust and smoke
reeks the smell and sound of war.
Son against son, daughter against daughter
makes the price of freedom savage.
For some, the price is death, for others,
it's a haunting reality of night terrors
that thrust through their very souls.
There is no security, no phone calls home,
no checking in with friends before their battles unknown.
Freedom is what it's all about,
freedom for you, so stand up and shout.
These men and women dare
to put their lives on the line because they care.
They fight for their country with honor and pride,
standing by each other, side by side.
Hold your head high, they're fighting for you.
Take nothing for granted, remember the price.
Support the troops and love our land,
and always know our troops are in God's hands.

Linda D. Calhoun
Plant City, FL

The Waitress and the Customer

This day with thoughts of nothing new,
decided to stroll the avenue.
Walked into this business place,
a restaurant known for its busy pace.
Noticed the waitress with the pretty face
tending to the pie case.
She asked, "How is your Valentine's day, Ace?"
Well now, struggled along the way,
trying to think of something to say.
Finally told her of my plight,
and pleaded with all my might.
"As of this Valentine's hour,
my love boat has no engine power."
"I shan't," she replied, "be your engine mechanic, you see."
Well now, it's plain to me;
this spring, when the grass is green with clover,
I'll ask the waitress to turn my engine over.

Leonard J. Trenkenschuh
Pueblo, CO

My Gift

This last year, an interesting one
Sometimes it's been tough, the rest has been fun

You have helped me in so many ways
A simple thank you is too little to say

Cards and flowers don't seem enough
Times the past year I've made your life rough

At times, I have been selfish and rude
Not ever thinking what I'm doing to you

Through it all, you have always been there
When I really needed it, you listened and cared

At all times, you saw a part that was good
Kept working with me when no one would

So life goes on, these moments won't last
Forgetting what happened, I won't repeat the past

I'm making you a promise, simple but true
To be the best I can be, my gift to you

Gary R. May
Edgewood, NM

A Small Token

For all of life's events
As time does pass us by.
For each word left unsaid,
But what was meant.
For laughter shared
And tears we cried.
Small token as it may be,
A passing thought
Or reason why.
For all of this,
There are no words,
But comfort now
As nothing else will do.
In this moment our hearts share,
I reminisce with you.

Maryann Campbell
Pleasant Hill, CA

Moccasins

The path is long and dusty
   Where moccasins tread
And prairie grass has faded
   In the desert heat

Precious water in summer
   Soothes parched lips and brow
Winter snow and chilly wind
   Alter the drum beat

Small moccasins
   Large moccasins
      New moccasins
         Worn moccasins

Haunting pulse of ancient drums
   Heard throughout the ages
In the hearts of a people
   Living brave and strong

No longer do moccasins dance
   Where many buffalo roam
But tread on reservations
   Where the path is long

Mary E. Bodor
Westminster, CO

It's My Life

It's my life, and I tried living it my way,
But God said, "You belong to me, so I'll have the last say."
I broke all His rules and refused to do His will.
He said, "That's okay, I love you still."
I lied, cheated, and even stole,
But guess what? He said, "I'll save your soul.
Just humble your heart and come unto me,
Oh, what a difference it will make, just wait and see."
So I tried Jesus and oh, what a change in my life,
No more anger, trouble, or strife.
I found peace oh, so brand-new.
If He did it for me, He'll do it for you.
I now know to whom I belong,
And to Him, I will always believe in this song—
"Jesus loves me, this I know, for the Bible tells me so."
So try Jesus, just give Him your heart.
You'll never be sorry that from Him you got your start.
He loves you now,
He will love you then—
He will love and be with you
To the very end.

Lucille E. Cotton
Raleigh, NC

Lessons to Learn from Haiti

May we learn lessons from the earthquake in Haiti.
Moreover, may we give gratitude to the volunteers,
There for 24/7 since the disaster started,
In addition to those who will assist at a later date/time.

All cultures and nations coming together to help
Those in need without discrimination.
They show us that peace is possible by caring, by love,
By trusting in God or a higher power.

Observe those Haitians under the rubble for many days
Who hoped and determined they would be rescued.
To those who died, but willed to live, and their suffering;
Pray they know joy and peace in their resting place.

Haitians have always been, mostly, living in poverty.
We have out own poverty areas.
No one should be living in poverty.
We need to build and teach with our strengths.
In addition, show how weakness can become strong.

When cultures and nations come together
Without discrimination, but with love and caring
And pledge to help make the world a better place;
Then all shall know the meaning of peace without poverty.

Jacqueline J. Adams
Maplewood, MN

Those Words

The things you said to me the other night,
I can't get out of my mind.
I was so happy that you said that,
That I laughed and then cried.
You always know how to take care of me
When something goes wrong.
You know how to make me smile
So I am never sad for long.
Those words you spoke to me
Make my heart love you more.
Now I know you love me just as much,
And I know we belong together for sure.
When we are together,
We have so much fun.
I couldn't help but smile when you looked at me and said,
"You are the one I love, you're my number one!"
If I wouldn't be as happy as I am today,
I don't know what I would do.
But now I know that I'm in love,
And I know that it's with you.

Brittany A. Brown
Hanover, PA

I chose to write this poem because of a few words someone said to me. He is the
reason I smile every day and the reason I can express my feelings in writing. He has
always stood by my side and helped me through everything. I am dedicating this
poem to the person I love the most and the person I call my best friend, Jonathan. I
love you and thank you for never giving up on me!

Missing You

Do you feel me?
I am there.
I am everywhere.
Go outside. Do you see me?
I am there.
I am everywhere.
Do not ever feel alone.
Close your eyes, touch your heart.

Do you feel me?
I am there.
I am everywhere.
We will be together once again,
But in the meantime,
Watch the flowers grow,
The animals run and play.
Listen to the birds sing.
Catch a big fish.
Go mushrooming, have cookouts.
Enjoy being together,
And remember,
I am there.
I am everywhere.

Tammy A. Bixler
Attica, IN

I have a close-knit family. We're always there for each other when needed. My mom enjoyed life and she loved the outdoors. She had the prettiest yard around with all the flowers she grew. She had raised so many different types of animals from little mice to a big emu. She made special times for everyone with holidays, birthdays, and family cookouts. This poem is dedicated to my mom. I lost my mom on October 8, 2008, but we will always have our memories. I love you, Mom!

Be an American

If you came to America
For a better way of life
Leave all that you are running from behind
Don't try to change this country
To your old ways of strife
Then a better life is surely what you'll find.

If you came to America
To make it better for your kids
Learn the language and try to be a friend
Make a home for your children
And keep them off the streets
Then you'll be welcome, on that you can depend.

If you came to America
To work and pay your way
Then this country will appreciate your toil
If you want to be an American
And you want to stay
Then the people will accept you and be loyal.

If you came to America
Looking for a better place
Work hard and do your best to make us strong
'Cause if you try to change us
To what you were, I know
We'll all need to find a better place to go.

Shirley A. Klotz
Garden City, KS

The Buzzing Bees of Dottingburg

A healing bee
We may not see.
If we think
It surely must be
A beautiful bee of pink and green, you see.

A singing bee of many voices
If we listen
We can hear
Songs of many choices.

A beautiful soprano bee
Can sing from Mississippi
To Europe, you see.

Mildred A. Futch
Waukegan, IL

The Forty-Fourth President

I remember the words spoken by Dr. Martin Luther King
"I have a dream, a dream that one day this nation
will rise up and live out the true meanings of its creed
that all men will be created equal"
It took the forty-fourth president to bring us to that one day
and a beautiful day it will forever be
A Black man stood up and proclaimed the word "Change"
and to be called President of the United States of America
"Yes, we can"
There is a lot of work ahead of us to do,
but our response should always be "Yes, we can"
Our characters will be challenged
Our integrity might be questioned
Yes, we can
United we stand on one common goal—change
We, the people, have spoken, our voices were heard
We salute this great country we call the United States
where change is possible and dreams come true
Thank you, Mr. President, for opening up the door
and removing the barriers, for out of many, we are one
Martin Luther King's dream lives on.

Dawn Hamilton
Uniondale, NY

Writing takes me to a place where I seek peace and contentment. When I look outside of myself and see the courage and spirit that families have shown through adversities and children who smile and still say thank you in spite of their illness and pain, they inspire me to write. My aim in life is to make a difference through my writings. Whatever you need to change in your life to bring forth your dreams, believe "Yes, I can." I have learned throughout the years our greatest blessings are found in ourselves.

The Bird's Tree

On the second day of 2010,
I chanced upon a tiny tree,
Which was alive
And overflowing
With tiny chirping birds.

I stopped to hear their song,
But they stopped to look at me.
As I walked slowly on,
They resumed their happy song.

Constance A. Warren
Detroit, MI

Brandon

You left me so soon without a goodbye.
Here I stand, scared and confused, with no will to try.
I miss you more than you will ever know,
But I know you are in Heaven watching His garden grow.
Inside and out, you had a great deal of pain,
Now you are in Heaven, smiling again.
We had laughs, shared tears, and you confided in me your greatest fear.
Who will I turn to if you're not here?
One thing is certain, I will never forget
My Superman, my angel, my best friend yet.

Holly E. Brown
Brownsville, PA

A First Night

I see traces of character embedded
Within my desire to understand her.
Our eyes examine each other.
We might lose after all
Traces of this morning.
A collaborative plot, too soon
Psychotic without apology.
Its simplicity is evident, arranged,
May paint character in the night sky.
Pastels tilt on the horizon.
With wine, the dream flows to the brain.
A red stain becomes the earth.
Life resumes in the stars
With bubbles to sexual things.
Like angels, we jump into the dark.
Our dreams in places of fear.
So far from the earth falls
In a transparent, positive state.
We laugh, happy with the past.

Thomas A. Phelan
Ramsey, NJ

Poetry has calmed my spirit after years of working as a policeman in the toughest precincts in New York City and then as a security consultant to the U.S. delegate in the Middle East (where we had altercations with terrorists and had our plane sabotaged at thirty-nine thousand feet). After writing my finest poem, I became mesmerized. I felt an enormous lightness of mind and spirit. I have been writing poetry ever since. My fourth book of poetry was published in 2009. I was featured in the *New York Times* "On Books" column; nominated for the Pushcart Prize in poetry; received an Author's Award from the New Jersey Institute of Technology; as well as being published in literary magazines throughout the U.S. I am eighty-two years old. I am a veteran of World War II and the Korean War. I am a grandmaster tenth Dan Black Belt in Korean karate and the 1975 kickboxing champion. I own a private detective agency and I am still writing.

Alone

I may be alone, but I am not as alone as one might think

I see the hurt and I see the tears they cry
I see the pain they endure to contain their "love"

I do not want that standing by my side
I do not want to host pain in my heart for some company

I may be alone, but I am not as alone as one might think

I want happiness every single day of my life
I do not want to settle for abuse and apologies every day

I am quite content with being alone at the beginning of my journey
I am perfectly happy striving for my future and success

I may be alone, but I am not as alone as one might think

I see myself with gifts of talent, advice, friends, and family
I am not alone as far as I can see

I see myself with a college degree, a job, a car,
and confidence in myself
I have many things to appreciate and look forward to

I may be alone, but I am not as alone as one might think

Brittany F. West
Holyoke, MA

Look at the Moon

Look at the moon
All barren cratered and scarred
Bearing the marks of a world
Destroyed beaten and pounded into dust
By celestial travelers
From beyond the edge of the universe
The lure of the moon beckons and calls
Heavenly bodies wandering blindly
Through our solar system
Drawing them to its
Seemingly lifeless dust gray bosom
Instead of allowing them to
Pulverize and devastate Mother Earth
The moon stands guard over us
Silent sentinel of the night
Protecting mankind from harm
Look at the moon
All barren cratered and scarred
Look at the moon
And see God

James R. Depp
Indianapolis, IN

You Can Hear the Angels Sing

You can hear the angels sing
when you hear the bells ring.
If you listen to each tone,
you will know you're not alone.
When the bells begin to peal,
in your heart, you'll know it's real.
You can almost hear their words.
They are singing to our Lord.

It's a miracle that's told
from the witnesses of old
of that blessed holy day;
by His birth, He came to save.
They are singing praise to Him.
Christ the Savior, He is king.
You can hear the angels sing
when the bells begin to ring.

Lady Sylvia A. Godfrey
Tavernier, FL

Detailing Winter

Another winter's dawn, I see,
With bits of snow, to fight the breeze,
Convinced the sun's too weak to share,
The Earth's resigned to bleak's aware.

My windows hate the steam inside,
Their shelter keeps all cold outside,
The shortened days and night's deep freeze
Are causing warmth to blanket me!

There's such a stir amidst my trees,
The wind is picking cones for me
As squirrels delight to find their store,
They're finding out their starve for more!

There's glory round that old oak tree,
When winter's thaw begins to see
A bin of leaves raked by its side,
Perhaps we'll use them just to hide!

This winter's season left heights of snow,
And giant drifts that come and go.
The river's crust of ice proves well
That many love to skate and tell!

In silence waits the season's change,
As each depart, we turn the page.
With springtime's best and clear blue skies,
The summer waits to lull us by.

Faye A. Deller
Wrightsville, PA

Pages of a Dream

Not a book, just pages in the mind,
"quiet" not an object that would make a sound,
just three white horses grazing on a green hilly pasture
on land that seems to be far away from a city or a town.

Not a house, a barn, no other animals, nor a picket fence.
A very bright sunny day, no sign of expression, only three
white horses grazing; this page didn't make much sense.

A page turned, not showing the motion of a quake or how
the green pasture had split in two; there is now a black hole
in the earth, no longer three horses, only two.

Between the black walls of the opened earth, one of the horses
fell into the black hole upside down.
The hole seemed bottomless, still no expression of sound.

Pages still turning, two horses remaining, one of them so
close to the edge a slight breeze would make him fall.
The third horse, secure on the green pasture,
had not been affected by the earth opening at all.

Maybe on the last page, the scene of two white horses,
an opened earth, a green pasture and the bright sun.
This dream has been interpreted into life's chances or warnings:
a lost, a possible, and a sure one.

Dorothy A. Burns
Lackawanna, NY

The Hour (of Tribulation)

We need You Lord
We need your awesome power
We need Your mercy and Your grace
To keep us from this hour

This hour that coming
Upon all this Earth
According to Revelation 3
In which You made a promise
To Your church
An open door to victory

I've witnesses Your awesome power Lord
And it's a marvelous thing to see
I was facing defeat and death
When You came and delivered me

We need You Lord
Without You we would fail
Like a ship in stormy waters
Lost and afraid without a sail.

Aron O. Wooten
Hooks, TX

My Caring About His Living

Yes Daddy the ambulance is here
So doctor his stroke has stopped
Yes Daddy I am right here
These are all his medications
Yes Daddy I know it's hard to talk
Okay nurse I can feed him
Yes Daddy you will get your strength back
He knows the therapy will be hard
Yes Daddy you are making progress
He does want to go to the dining room
Yes Daddy we'll get a different walker
You respect his decision to go home
Yes Daddy you might need the wheelchair
He wants to cook his own breakfast
Yes Daddy your handicap bathroom is a plus
I encourage him to exercise with his walker
Yes Daddy I will call your barber
He works crossword puzzles every day
Yes Daddy I miss Mama too
He says there is pain all the time
Yes Daddy that's on your grocery list
He doesn't like getting out anymore
Yes Daddy I can do that for you
He misses his independence
Yes Daddy I love you too
I choose to care about his living

Christine M. Leckbee
Odessa, TX

9-11-2001

Beautiful skyscrapers, the Twin Towers as they were called
those from all places in the world who saw these were awed
On this fateful day, the Trade Center's work had begun
The day of market trading would soon be on the run
As early dawn was breaking in our states of the west
New York's day had started while western states were at rest
When from the skies heinous murderers took captive a jet
At eight forty-six a.m., New York would feel such fret
With all innocent aboard this plane aimed for the tower
Hitting the North Tower, creating death and such terror
In minutes, the South Tower was hit with deadly aim
Horror our country felt as more lives this jet, too would claim
Then monsters with more innocent aboard charged the Pentagon
Many lives, many families stolen by this great wrong
O'er Pennsylvania, great souls fought for the lives of others
These heroes took this jet down, saving more sisters and brothers
Four planes were taken, four used as a weapon against freedom
Our president spoke as our tears, our hearts, our calm
We ache for loved ones lost by the terrorists' treacherous deed
Shown were our heroes, thus we shall not succumb to heinous greed
We shall endure, this nation under God, America!
And we ask again this day, dear God, bless America!

Rae Ann Barton
Rancho Santa, Margarita, CA

From a Mother to a Daughter's Heart

As i get older let me always try to live my life to the fullest. To do as much as I can. For life is a precious gift. Time given to live is now . . . not later. There is time to rest when I die.

No matter how sick the Doctor shall tell me that I am, let me try to remember to listen past those words and hear the doctor tell me how much longer I have left to live.

Let me remember there are people whom I now have time to see and meet. And no matter how bad I may feel, utilige the moment I am given in life to get out and find socialization. As most of my life has been spent wishing I had time to do the things I have now been given the chance to do.

Let me pass down my family values and morals. Let me teach my child love comes from the heart. A relationship is based on what you do together in life as individual people sharing one life together, not in how you have lived your life together trying to share it as one.

Let me remember the laughter my child and I have had and may share. Let me set aside the tears they may have helped me to shed along the way. Let me remember the tears of joy.

Let me be strong enough to admit where I have made mistakes in my life if confronted,
and remember I was not always nor am I perfect beyond the human form. Mistakes are the creation of wisdom to come.

Let me live my life through the eyes of my greatest hero and teacher. My mentor. My mother. And as I get older. Let me continue to see life as a beautiful gift.

Let me capture the perfect picture of living the same as she always did and always will. As thought the eyes of the life she has left behind. She will forever be embedded within me. In her footsteps forever I will live.

Shana L. Boulton
Burlington, IA

Until Your Love

I never imagined . . .
That excitement could bewitch me so
That the sun could seem brighter,
The flowers more fragrant, the moonlight softer
That music could fill up my soul
That I could laugh with such abandon
That the kiss could taste honey sweet
That passion could leave me feeling heady and intoxicated
I never imagined . . .
That I would pause to find the beauty within
That I would want to sing all day and then dance all night
That I would extend my heart
That I eagerly would anticipate each new dawn
That I would be captivated by kindness
That I would celebrate life so
No, I never imagined . . .
Until your love.

Ricarda M. Payne
Culver City, CA

I deeply feel that poetry is the most perfect way to both express and treasure the timeless gifts that life offers each of us—love, friendship, beauty, passion, humor, trust, sensitivity, challenge, hope, joy, inner growth, and spirituality. While writing poetry is my hobby, it is also my salvation!

January 2010—Haiti

First the tremors
Rumbles
Tumbles
Dust
From the Earth's crust
Losing thousands of her country's members
Broken concrete
Pain
At first, no rain
Prayers
From the sayers
Some buried very deep
Most countries rally
Water
From the Father
And food sent
For all souls, the intent
Recipients grateful, without dally
Many children and adults will transport
To other island parts
And to other countries for fresh start
Continued land quakes
Stay outside for own sake
All this, reminder of everyone's human sort.

Marcia A. Bianchi
Mt. Vernon, WA

Through the Eyes of an Angel

The angel's
wings spread
ever so gently
across the night sky.
Her beauty
was more breathtaking
than every
flower and blue
sky combined.
And then suddenly, in the
silence of the night,
sadness over came her
as she looked upon our world.
Tears filled her
eyes and trickled down
her face like a sad,
gloomy rain.
I could feel her heart breaking
as she cried for those
who have lost hope,
and for those who
have lost their way.

Christina M. Zagami
Kinzers, PA

A Walk in the Woods

If only the woods would wait
A moment stand unchanged
I would go for a walk
In the first color of fall

There would be an interruption
Time caught in filtered sunlight
Mosaic yellow and red moss

The shadows would reign with mystery
I would look for small stones
Tumbled into marbles
In motionless streams

When movement came again
I would shed leaves
Like trees fall
Into the cradle of impermanence

Albert J. Capovilla
Rancho Cordova, CA

The Tree of Life

Through the depths of a tree, there are rings of life
that flow around each other in different
motions that resemble emotions.
It resembles the world and how everything
begins a young and fragile soul.
If you can look within the trunk of the tree,
you may be able to understand
how it helps everything and everyone to live from day to day.
You can enjoy the story that the tree contains
as each day begins in the sunlight that generates
growth throughout time,
where weather has helped it to develop into
an adult over the years.
Then each evening to lay to rest under
the star-glazed sky surrounding the pie we call the moon.
All souls throughout the world can unite together
relating to the tale of a lifetime we have learned from nature.

Carrie L. Stinson
Crystal, MN

Picking Flowers

I have for you, my darling
a nice bouquet of thoughts,
with colors like the orchids
and some forget-me-nots.

I'll write for you, my angel,
here, a fresh bouquet.
With lovely words, I'll tell you
what I can't seem to say.

I'll share the lovely thoughts
that I have just of you,
and tell you of my wishes
that I know can't come true.

The greatest plans, my darling,
on your sweet dreams, I've built,
and this bouquet I give you,
my love, will never wilt.

Joseph H. Sollers
Rodeo, NM

I do not write poetry or construct lines of verse and rhyme. I only write down what
my heart tells me or wants to say to one I may love. It is only luck that it comes out
in metered rhyme. I would like to share my heart with you.

The Lady Slipper

The lovely lady slipper
She grows among the tents
Of hundreds and hundreds of mushrooms
She bows, and sometimes bends.

Her bog bellows
Songs by gifted frogs
They sing and eat tiny bugs
Well hidden in the logs.

Long worms burrow
Round holes that have no light,
For they live in dark circles,
And their day is never bright.

A thunderous herd of mosquitoes
Came flying through the mist,
And those pesky beast annoyed the lady,
Their daggers try to sting!

The slippered mouth opened wide,
Swallowing the tiny beast,
And if you come back again,
I'll have another feast!

Dorothy L. Harding
Strawberry Plains, TN

When I create a poem, my thoughts drift back to my American Indian friend Two Mountain. Although his physical presence has long passed, his spirit still lingers in my thoughts today. In my quiet moments when I write, I ask myself, what would he say and how would he say it?

O' Cedar Tree

O' cedar tree, what do you see?
Do you impart more soul than heart;
More than beyond the very bond
Of heart 'n soul or rock 'n roll?
O' cedar tree, what do you see?

How years do change and rearrange
The hill and dale, even the swale
Of Man's expression, nature's impression,
Awash with scars gouges and mars?
O' cedar tree, what do you see?

I'd like to think it's safe to drink,
To plant and grow and weed and hoe;
Fertile land lending a hand
To life's renewal—the proper fuel.
O' cedar tree, do you feel glee?

Greenhouse effect, the world's a wreck,
Ozone depletion, atomic fission,
Increased pollution and radiation,
Improper diction, Karma and fiction,
Warring and chaos—an albatross?

O' cedar tree, what do you see?

Jeannie F. Locke
Auburn, ME

The Cross Within

When we think of our God breathing stars
From His mouth to give us light,
We think of all His creation being just right.
We think of our bodies and how
He created us to move and go,
But have we ever thought of how
He made all of this so?

Laminin, which holds one cell of our body to the next,
Without them, we would fall apart.
Our God knew all this before
He began to start.
Because they are in the shape of a cross,
And we live as Christians should,
He will always be with us showing
His love and care,
And taking us to Heaven
Where we can be with Him up there.

Janis B. Drinnon
Knoxville, TN

I wrote my first poem to comfort my mother-in-law when my father-in-law passed away in 1977 as a thank you for her words of comfort when my own mother passed away in 1970. The first poem was published in 1996, the first of many poems to be published and receive several awards. I have always enjoyed the finer things in life and nature, especially those that are spiritually uplifting and bring beauty to the soul. My family has always come fist in my life. I try to reflect my religious faith through the spiritual nature of my poems. "In His Care," a book of my inspirational poems and selected Bible verses, was published in 1998.

God Has a Purpose for My Life

God has a purpose for my life
more meaningful than just being a mother and a wife.

I'll tell you why I feel this way
in this little poem that I wrote today.
Although I love my children, and I love my husband too,
I still feel very strongly
that there's more I'm called to do.

I'm not the same now since I was born again,
I've become a new creation since He saved my soul from sin.
"Ambassador for Christ" is the title that was given to me
when I was born into the heavenly royal family.
I publish good news of the gospel to all who want to know.

Working, singing, laughing, playing,
dancing, preaching, writing, and praying . . .
I know my purpose now, and I'm very glad!

'Tis the most exciting experience that I have ever had!
Working for Him from now on till my time on Earth is through,
that's God's purpose for my life. . . .
That's what I'm going to do.

Dedra J. Nowlin
Siloam Springs, AR

You Are

You are the prism that refracts
The light of my late afternoon
And renders it chromatic.

You are the grace notes that transform
My languishing recessional
To cadences ecstatic.

You are a wondrous pianist
Who plays the *Pathetique* Sonata,
But a greater wonder yet,
You are the *Appassionata*.

You are the cyclamen that flares
When other flowers bow.
You are the fabled bliss to come,
Miraculously here and now.

Abner E. Shimony
New Haven, CT

"You Are" celebrates my marriage at an advanced age to Manana Sikic in New Haven, Connecticut on the vernal equinox of 2005.

Mussolini

In Italy,
little boot,
condition strode
down a
second millennial
road
to goad
diverse nations
into war,
polished up
on no
particular
treading
the adjacent
and the far
till on the heels
of dust
was seen he,
hung-sprung
like linguine,
the axiomatic
meany,
Mussolini.

Richard Charles Thayer
Turners Falls, MA

Taylor

Do you know how very much I miss you?
It is less than a year that you've been gone.
The hurt was so deep that I didn't know what to do.
In my grief you came to me with "Welcome home."

I saw you there all dressed in white,
Peace shining on your handsome face.
Then I knew you would forever be all right.
You were reaching to me from a beautiful place.

I reached for you, but our Father said, "Not yet."
But you let me see that you would be there;
You would be waiting, and I will never forget
The peace I saw in that land so fair.

I praise God that we will soon be together,
The trials, tears gone then, and no pain.
He will take them away forever and ever.
There pure peace and joy will ever reign.

Kathylene Dusenberry
Oskaloosa, IA

Iron Ribbons, Poison Petals

Iron ribbons entangled my limbs.
Poison petals burn my skin.
Constrained in your personal hell
Of fiery pastels.

Iron ribbons tighten around my neck.
Poison petals take away my very breath.
Enjoying your fun?
But I understand your game has just begun.

Iron ribbons cripple me in every way.
Poison petals of a deadly bouquet.
Take your time,
You seem to think you're so sublime.

Well, not any longer.
You will soon realize you are not stronger.

Iron ribbons break.
Poison petals disintegrate.

Take your time,
Just walk away.
I will heal my broken flesh of yesterday.

Amanda L. Bond
Green Valley, AZ

True Parents

True parents, I need you,
I don't know
what else I can do.
I really need parents,
That I can look up to.
True parents, your heart,
embraces each one of us.
Your love for mankind
and God really
warms my heart.
True parents,
you're my parents,
you understand and
care for us, it's true.
In the deepest struggles
we go through,
you're the ones that we turn to.
Sometimes we feel that we can no longer go on.
The struggles are too
great and the goals, just too far.
That's when we seek you most,
our hearts and hands are
outstretched to you.
Forgive me, Father, that I'm not
enough for you.
Forgive me, dear Mother,
that I'm not more like you!

Diane E. Ryan
Staten Island, NY

Morning Awakening

As I awake in the morning

I immerse myself into
the new day

The dawn is breaking

I am arising

Central activities
of the mind

conclude and coerce
into a ray of
sunshine

I melt in the glory

of all I am adoring

Oh sweet dreams

of saturating realms

Arlene A. Ascenzo
Torrington, CT

The Fade of Winter

Breezes warm the sleeping trees while gusting to and fro,
Falling raindrops replace the beautiful flakes of snow.
Zephyrs awaken shrubs and brushes while murmuring about,
Calling roots and bulbs beneath the soil,
"Wake up, it's time to come out."
Slivers of green begin to peek through spiritless brown fields,
Bringing the miracle of life to the soul of the Earth.
We're eagerly awaiting the annual rebirth
Of spring; it's almost here.

Mildred M. Staten-Wallace
Baltimore, MD

I Vow

Tyler, I vow to you
my heart, my love,
I'll always stay true.
For you, my love, this is what I'll do.
I vow a smile every day,
and happiness that'll never fade.
My lips to kiss whenever you please,
and my hand to hold when in need.
A simple vow I give to you
for now, later, and forever, too.
Tyler, my love this is what I'll do.
I vow my love, my heart, and my life to you.

Jessica R. Pase
Baltimore, MD

Ezekiel Saw the Wheel

Ezekiel saw the wheel.
He saw visions of God.
Ezekiel dropped to his knees.
He knew it was real.
Do you believe in the Bible
Or do you just warm church seats?
I saw five silver UFOs.
They were below the clouds.
Radar could not touch!
San Francisco was beautiful.
I was standing on the balcony
On Linden Street
Smiling from to ear to ear.
It's a strange universe.
Silently, they went away.
I hope to see them another day.

Mary L. Buggs
Oakland, CA

Courage

There comes a time in life where good things come and go
But all your job did was put on a hell of a show
Everyone had looked up to you
I guess that wasn't enough to pull through
You always went above and beyond
This had made time for you and your team to build a stronger bond
I will say that you had a good run
But there were some things that just couldn't be done
This was no one's fault
Unfortunately, you still had to walk
You did have some perks
But you deserved all of the works
You came home with a box
That is when all of our hearts just stopped
Yes, a change had came
But that will not change or end our family name

Crystal A. LaSorsa
Poughkeepsie, NY

Mother Nature

Waves come gleefully in to play with the sand,
The wind whispering in and out of the clouds
Trees with their leaves reaching out clapping their hands
Spreading joy all over the land
Flowers blooming here and there
Like little faces sending sweet aromas everywhere
The fog playing games with the mist,
Then suddenly like a giant fist, out of nowhere came
A thunderous roar, splitting the skies
With bolts of lightning like spitting fire everywhere
Raindrops falling like tears rolling down from the heavens above
The sun playing peek-a-boo disappeared till there was no more ado
Mother Nature is not smiling now,
Her children playing havoc all around
Telling all to beware; if you mess with her, she will make you pay
The beautiful waves will come roaring in,
Beating the sand most of the day
Winds start to churn into spinning whirls of dust,
Picking things up every which way
For miles they will twirl, then suddenly fall where they may,
Rain falling to and fro
Slashing and splashing pellets of drops
Like tiny pebbles thrashing around and around
Which seems like forever
The sun, not smiling, said that is enough!
We do not want anymore
Her rays flung out in dismay, flaying around every which way
Mother Nature said with a sigh,
Let the sun shine again, let no more tears fall from the sky
Let the waves play games with the sand once more
May the wind no longer blow, but turn into a breeze,
Kissing the flowers and making them bloom more than before
Clouds like marshmallows floating in the air

Like soft cotton balls swinging in the sky
The fog and mist disappeared, we know not where
We know mother nature has much more in store,
Like snow, tornadoes, and hurricanes,
Floods that can tear over the land
Drenching and pouring water everywhere, she can dry up our land,
Cracking and dying of thirst; remember, she will not always be fair
Treat her gently and she will be as gentle as she can

Jean M. Franzone
Macedonia, OH

My poems are inspired by my sixteen grandchildren and my twenty-five great-grandchildren. Their inquisitive minds and wonderful imaginations gave me the ideas for my poetry. I will dedicate this poem to them.

They Talk . . . Do They Listen?

John wanted us to imagine
that there were so much
better days ahead
He nudged us
from his piano
telling us how easy it will be
He reaches o'er the wavelengths
on the path they trod together
Roger's there to meet today
with world war on his mind
as how his father met his end
his thoughts are sung so gracefully
No one kills the children anymore
Both want the world to be
free from terror, war, and prejudice
Our Savior taught to follow
the same tune these minstrels sing
but look around our
sad, sad world
Peace on the horizon
yet the sun has set.

Jerry N. Cushman
Indian Head, MD

God's Handiwork

The God of this great universe
Is not hard to get to know
One can clearly picture Him
In the delicate flakes of snow

In the stars that shine so bright at night
Or a rainbow after the rain
In a gentle breeze caressing the trees
In a hymn with a haunting refrain

God's handiwork is everywhere
Revealing His love for all
Spilling over the whole wide world
Like a glorious waterfall

He poured His beauty over the Earth
To display His caring heart
Welcoming all who are listening
To draw near and become a part

How to respond to this generous God
It is up to us to decide
Hopefully with a resounding yes
For in us He wants to abide

Marcie E. McNutt
Amherst, NY

Grandmother, I Miss You

God lives here, she says.
We enter a canopy of leaves
to protect us from the rain.
I spot a bed of pine needles for a nap,
a gurgling spring offers us refreshment.
Her eyes take on a lively sparkle and
she invites me to dance with her.

She smiles to welcome a butterfly
landing on her strong forearm.
There are no wrinkles left in her face
while walking in the forest.
Her steps are exactly placed—
just as her father had taught her
when she walked with him as a child.
She takes her breath from the Earth.

Birds fly into the air and I clap my hands—
with joy. Shafts of light flicker through
the trees. God lives here.
This is the freedom she holds close.
Grandmother, I will miss you always.

Sarah C. Wolters
Staunton, VA

My gentry grandmother developed a special bond with me since my mother, brother, and I lived with her and Granddad during World War II. My grandmother took special delight in dressing me up. I was her welcome kitchen helper. She proudly took me to church with her, all scrubbed with ribbons in my hair. The foundation for my life was laid where God was a natural presence and prayer a way of life. I am a senior citizen now. With thanks, I leave this poem as a legacy of our relationship.

Liberty Under God

This nation, our land
You show us greatly
Your caring hands of love
Your mercy extended
Protecting our country
Defending our borderlines
Your orders from Heaven
That forge a strong tower
A pure shield over our lives
Attentive are Your ears
That readily listen
To our petitioning
You faithfully answer
With Your gentle kindness
A beautiful love for all
And we believe that You
Are truly always there
Yes, united, we shall stand

Betty J. Ekhator
Hyattsville, MD

Opus

Hear the sparrow
Grace the heavens with his joy.
Oh, radiant firmament
This day of glory echoes round.
The skies are ringing blue
Above the vibrant grass
On which we stand
As momentary reflections
Of immortality.
We are the visions
God has dreamed
And sent abroad
As rapture for a pulsing universe,
For in the singing of our souls,
His laughter ripples joyously
Between the heartbeats of eternity
And sets the cosmos dancing.

Marian A. Evans
Fort Littleton, PA

Where Happiness Dwells

Yesterday does not stay; the seasons turn.
The months and years melt away.
The rosy cheeks will fade—
Soon it is autumn in our heart.

During this twilight time of life,
We will probably become cognizant
Of the tendency we always had
To become caught up in the rush of things,
And it may seem that many of our needs
And desires have only been partially fulfilled.

We realize that we did not take enough time
To listen to the rain falling on the steps,
To hear the song of the wild goose,
Or to observe the wildflowers in the forest.

We need to pay closer attention
To that inner voice within,
To take care of those small things
That keep our heart entranced
And realize that happiness is found in minutiae—
The flickering light of a candle,
The gentle rustling of leaves,
The innocent expression on a baby's face,
Or a child's laughter of joyfulness.

Gerald E. Pettus
Sacramento, CA

Red Sky in the Morning

The sky belched clouds of thunder,
Stabbing lights incised the dark,
Spears from Jupiter, an angry god,
But no rain fell, not yet,
Gulf waters rose in tribute
Beneath an ominous towering spout.

Pets shivered, needing comfort,
While sheltered people waited out in watch
Then clouds burst their burden
A battery of sodden, strafing bullets struck
New gullies stated dry land,
Washing winds-swept streets, drenching torrid air.

The savage storm stilled suddenly,
The ground sighed mistily as the town took back its tempo,
The deluge past and done.

Was this swift-moving morning storm a signal flare?
Was it forerunner of fiercer ones to come?
Where sparse shelters overcrowd with nowhere to run?
A warning call to challenged change,
For living in an afternoon before the fall of night?
Friends, seek a strong emerging sun for rainbow-hunting.

Patricia E. Vigneau
Spring Hill, FL

Walk with Me

Lord, grant me the
Courage to stand on my own
When all my world,
Thy love has gone!
Lord, grant me the strength
To hold my head up high,
Put a smile on my face
When my eyes want to cry.
When my mind's in turmoil,
Despair, my friend,
Show me the wisdom to know
It will all end.
Walk with me, Lord,
Show me the way.
Help me get through it
Till the next sent day.
I know I will survive
If You lead me along,
And stand by my side
Till all's where it belongs.

Dennis C. McClendow
Pasadena, CA

The Windmill

The windmill stood there idle,
Two blades lay on the ground,
Remembering in silence
When they'd gone round and round.
It used to be majestic,
While pumping oh, so grand
The water for the livestock,
The farmer's helping hand.

The rural water district
Throughout the countryside,
Had made it no more needed,
Progress had turned the tide.
A passing motorist wondered,
And thought how sad it seemed,
Would love to see it pumping.
The windmill stood and dreamed:

"If magic could repair me,
The wind could have its way.
I'd love to pump fresh water,
If only for a day."
In time, the weather threatening,
The windmill will be gone,
And only in our memories,
The windmill will live on.

Betty-Rae Starks
Anthony, KS

The words to this poem tumbled from my mind as I reflected on having seen one in a pasture one day near where I grew up on a farm. In those days, they were essential, for the rural water lines had not come into existence yet. I see that particular windmill just about every month as I have occasion to drive that direction, and yes, it has missing blades, just as the poem states.

238

A World of Difference

Fighting is not the answer
When will our leaders understand
When will people come to realize
Fighting destroys their native land
Although technology has made us smarter
It's left us vulnerable in every way
Private lives, no longer private
Identities stolen every day
Global warming, a big problem
Not much relief in sight
What will it take
All this wrong to make it right
I remember when the grass was greener
No toxins in the air
Pollution wasn't heard of
Much beauty everywhere
Just a teen back in the fifties
No need to lock the door
Today, a world of difference
What are we fighting for

June S. Sunkes
Lynnwood, WA

A Simple Dream

All I want is the wind in my hair,
And a swing to rock me when I feel sad
An open field, far away is what I dream about
A place unknown to Man
Pure, peaceful, left untouched
Someday I'll find that place, that field in the sun
A dream I constantly run toward, yearning to grasp
A fantasy close to my heart
That place where grass sways gently,
Dancing to nature's music
In that dream, the field accepts and loves me
As I am, and I can let my hair down with
No one around to watch,
Yes, it's just Jah and me
Yes, that is freedom, freedom to just be
To cry when the tears come, to sing a song
That is now unknown to me
To run and dance about freely
That peaceful field where life
And the future stresses just fade away
A swing, an open field basking in the sun
A gentle breeze, my freedom, to which I daily run
Where you are, I do not know, but I hold on to your dream
I promise not to let you go

Serena Galli
Honesdale, PA

New Mellie

It's early in the morning
The world is waking up.

All the birds are singing
I dare not interrupt.

The geese, the hawks, the blackbirds
Are all ignoring me.

But I'm looking out the window
Enjoying what I see.

The fluffy little woodpecker
Is sharping up his bill

As old Mr. Sun
Is peeping over the hill.

The fog slides off the water
Propelled by an unseen hand.

Soon I'll have to join the world
And take my daily stand.

But in this hour of early dawn
Before the world is up

I saw a little bit of God
As He was sprucing up.

Jane J. Jenkins
Aspen, CO

Love Trumpets

Often through these God-blessed days,
I think of beautiful passion we shared
in the garden of just two flowers.
Oh, aching heart, why beat swiftly
when the nightingale calls her name?
Oh, heart, what lovely times she and I had
upon the throne of virtue.
Her sweetness was all about my lips, face, brow,
and my mortal soul.
In my dreams of passion, the ray from her smile
pierces through the opaque objects of my loneliness
where only she is loving me.
I need her in the beginning of my offs and the tiedness of my ends.
If I was some super-mortal with universal power,
I would only leave her as she was mine
in the sweetness of togetherness.
Nay, my love will never die.
Her love is in the bottom of my heart
and her kiss at the peak of my cry.
Mannerism is so rare for me to find upon others.
Oh, God, please let us meet once more,
and the love we have will last throughout our mortal life
and still go on to You,
the giver of all virtue, love, passion.

Rogers E. James
St. Albans, NY

Seasons with a Reason

No one could ever out-give God, the Father of us all;
The gift He gave many years ago is priceless, endless love.

The birth of Christ, be very wise, don't let His name escape—
The proof of the gift God offers you is more to celebrate.

It is to rejoice, be happy, give honor, and praise God;
His Son waits patiently to hear your humble, faithful call.

The gift God offers is there—accept or reject, your choice;
Believe God raised Christ from the dead and you will rejoice.

Not just for the season, for the reason, for you will never die;
The life is spirit, it lives within, it's how you will survive.

Not just during your life on Earth, but forevermore you'll be
In an endless life with God and Christ for all eternity.

Josephine W. Bannister
Sandston, VA

Are You Listening, God?

Are You listening, God
As I cry out to You?
What do You want me to do?
My world is no longer a place of solitude.

Are You listening, God?
Your people are in trouble
And don't know what to do
In this torn and troubled world.

Are you listening, God?
I want to know.
God said, pray and love each other,
And I will grant you solitude

Zelma L. Coleman
Athens, OH

Since I Met You, I'm Not Afraid

Look, God, I have never spoken to You,
But now I want to say, how do You do?
You see, God, they told me You didn't exist,
And like a fool, I believed all this.

Last night from a shell hole, I saw Your sky.
I figured right then that they had told me a lie.
Had I taken time to see things You made,
I'd have knowing they weren't calling a spade a spade.

I wonder, God, if You'd shake my hand.
Somehow, I feel that You will understand.
Funny I had to come to this hellish place
Before I had time to see Your face.

Well, I guess there isn't much more to say,
But I'm sure glad, God, I met You today.
I guess the "zero hour" will soon be here,
But I'm not afraid since I know You're near.

The signal! Well, God, I have to go.
I like You lots, this I want You to know.
Look now, this will be a horrible fight.
Who knows, I may come to Your house tonight.

Though I wasn't friendly to You before,
I wonder, God, if You'd wait at Your door.
Look, I'm crying! Me, shedding tears!
I wish I had known You these many years.

Well, I have to go now, God, goodbye.
Strange; since I met You, I'm not afraid to die.

Bertha M. Lotzer
Balch Springs, TX

245

Precious Smile

What does it cost to cast a smile
On all the people you meet?
Nothing at all, it's just
A simple way to greet.

I get such a warm feeling
Deep in my heart
When I look into their eyes
And know to some
It's such a great surprise.

What are they thinking?
Do they feel as I do, that all of this makes my day?
I hope this day is complete for them, too.
Happiness is better than being blue.

So try this precious commodity
That's free to all on Earth.
Next time you get a chance,
Look into someone's eyes,
Crack a smile, and make your day worthwhile.

Josephine E. Martino
Springfield, PA

Spaced Out

Gadgets to help with the cooking are needed more and more
To help prepare those dishes the family clamors for.
The mixer and the toaster, the toaster oven, too—
The Crock Pot does the cooking when the microwaves won't do.
The processor works its magic for shredding and to slice.
Then we got the Vita Mix—we thought that it would dice.
The breadmaker's so handy, so's the speedy coffee pot.
Pasta maker, popcorn popper, fondue pot and wok—
Pressure cooker, indoor grill, a sealer for the bags;
Waffle iron, coffee grinder, dispenser for the tags.
The steamer and the skillet, the double boiler, too,
The canner's now electric, a deep fryer that is new.
Ice crusher is so useful, the blender is a must,
Sandwich maker's needed to brown it to a crust.
The radio informs me when the TV's not in use,
CD player gives me songs when not listening to the news.
I marvel at my helpers as each stands in its place,
But when I start to fix a meal, I find I have no space!

Betty W. Bishop
Hampton, FL

I was born in West Virginia nearly eighty-five years ago. I graduated from high school in Pennsylvania and worked on airplanes during World War II for Bell Aircraft in Niagara Falls, New York. I moved to Florida in 1945 and got married in 1946. We had four fantastic sons who each have equally fantastic wives. We have nine grandchildren and "almost" ten great-grandchildren. My hobbies include reading, writing, and doll collecting. Writing poetry about people and things I know; I started years ago. This poem is self-explanatory. God is my first love and all else follows closely. My ninety-six-year-old sister, Naomi, has been my lifelong buddy, proofreader, and encourager. I am blessed!

247

A Touch of Nature

On a dew-sparkled blade
A silvery web is spun
The artist's abode.

Morning glories climb
Over topping trellis wall
Displaying splendor.

Robin redbreast comes
The heralding of spring
Winter lingers on.

Sunlit, rolling fields
Fresh mown hay scents breeze wafted
Sweetness of autumn.

Wondering afar
Searching for identity
Which was left behind.

In a thunderstorm
Beating rain and rushing wind
Ah, powerless Man.

Beatrice M. Gartee
Lagrange, GA

My inspiration is nature, every phase of it. There is something wonderful to behold. It is exciting! I am a retired teacher of English, with a master's degree in English and education. My family is supportive in all my pursuits. I like to write, read, and travel. My husband and I lived about six months a year in an RV roaming Mexico, Canada, and the United States as the wanderlust called.

Naked

Lying naked by your side,
Bare for you to see,
Exposed of all the demons
That hide inside of me.

Unveiled of all my pretense,
Stripped of my fortress walls,
Open for your discovery,
I hear your heartfelt calls.

Uncovered are many emotions
That live beneath my skin.
An eternity empty of passion,
I now long to let you in.

Sheltered within your arms,
Blanketed by your affection,
Surrounded by your love,
Our hearts united in perfection.

Theresa A. Bucci
Boca Raton, FL

Poignant and Humorous Memories

When one of us forgot, someone else remembered.
We were able to reclaim our lives because someone with
shared memories had saved it and given it back.
We never knew where life would take us, so we prized what we had:
phone call, chance meeting, old photo album pages Kinko-copied.
We thanked God for our shared history.
Some moved to faraway places, and we kept them all—
our friends of old, they are gold!
Hamburgers and fries equal saturated fat,
back in the '40s who'd have "thunk" that!
Now cholesterol's a "no-no" for the artery,
so no more desserts that are sweet and buttery.
Oh, woe be to us with high blood pressure,
we must forgo meats and salt for salads that are fresher.
Favorite recipes concoct visions over which we drool and chat—
just as gourmets compare and "chew the fat."
From fifty years ago, the progression of food to us today (1997)
boils down to a remembrance of taste, texture, and aroma,
which seemingly says
visualizations are the only healthy, safe, and best ways.

Frances I. Smith
Anchorage, AK

Before his fiftieth class reunion, I phoned and asked a classmate from kindergarten to high school to sing his "funny" song, I forgot some of the words. His voice was hoarse, speech barely discernible, but I insisted he sing his song. Though ill, he was still a character. His singing was raspy and whispery, but warm-up improvement made the time and words actually sound good! We laughed, chatted, enjoyed the moment, and said goodbye. Two months later, he was dead. I thank God I savored that shared moment, a 100% in the now gift—indelible memory.

Box of Ashes

My mind is a box

Inside the box is a garden
Inside the garden is winter

Your ghost is a great gnarled tree
sprawling bare black limbs
against the sky

The sky is the color of ashes
I held your ashes in my hand

I hear your ashes rustling
like the echoes of leaves
that have long since fallen
I hear your ashes rustling
like whispers in my mind

My mind is a box

Elizabeth S. Caudy
Skokie, IL

barfly

and they haven't left their current phase
except to recap the good ol' days
when responsibility was something more
than anyone was ready for
not so much has really changed
all that's changed is why
they used to drink for pride
and now they drink to die
my barfly, my barfly
i won't ever ask you why.

Zack Mueller
Cresskill, NJ

The Wait

Lament thy soul's fate.
What rocky shores
crash beneath, retaliate
and beckon thy body forward
and back!
Instead, wait
and tearing,
proclaiming thy profligate state,
and waiting to
lament thy soul's cold fate.

Jovita L. Austin
Tacoma, WA

Watchful Eye and Steady Prayer

Within her arms she held him
So very, very tight,
And rocked him oh, so gently,
All through the night.
With dawn's bright glowing,
She smiled at his sweet face
'Cause sleepy eyes had told her
His fever had been erased.
All night she as anxious,
Sick was her baby son.
Watchful eye and steady prayer
Made her task well done.

Laura B. Lorenz
So. James, MN

I am eighty-eight years old and am a widow. I love to write. For the past thirty years, I have written stories and poetry and also whatever comes from the tip of my pen. When our son was a few months old, he had colic. The doctor said to keep rocking him and that would help, so I believe that was what inspired me to write the poem "Watchful Eye and Steady Prayer." I hope you enjoyed it as much as I enjoyed writing it.

Sweet Willie

Sweet Willie was born in a different time
God picked the best jewel He could find
For she had a mission and purpose in life
Some filled with love and some filled with strife
Little did she know the time would come
On the rich folks' farm a son would be born
The lady of the house needed someone to care
Someone to care for the child she would bear
She picked Sweet Willie none other would do
Sweet Willie took care of the lad as he grew
The bond of great love grew with limits few
Everyone knew Big Ern loved Sweet Willie too
As the years went by they leaned on each other
He cared for her like she was his mother
Fortunes he made and fortunes he gave
But through all the years Sweet Willie stayed
Then came the time when Ern passed away
To "The Upper Room" Sweet Willie would say
Alas! Sweet Willie could no longer stay
Ern needed her in "The Upper Room" that day.

Sally Ray
Palestine, TX

254

From Seed to Flower

You once were a seed in the earth
Consumed by enormous dirt

Somebody came along and saw you athirst
And gave water and your seed did burst

You started to grow but then you stopped
Through the weeds you constantly fought

Then along came the Master's hand
And He tended your flower according to His plan

He tore away the weeds and tilled the soil
Now your flower can really grow

Your flower stands out among the rest
Because Jesus glorified you while you did your best

So praise God for what you are
And you will always go very far

Mary E. Dandridge
Seaside, CA

Rocking Chair of Loneliness

I sit in a chair of loneliness, thinking of days gone by
Joy once filled my heart, now empty, but do not want to die
I sit in this chair of loneliness, feeling much despair
If only one hand to hold me tight, one who really cares
Looking out the window of time
Like a clock that ticks and chimes
With hours passing by, I take in stride
Wishing my loved ones were by my side
I would like to laugh and talk
Instead of this rocking chair that rocks
God, hear my prayer, I know You hear
Doors to open wide, to see loved ones by my side
My heart will rejoice, washing away the pain
In this chair of loneliness, will never be the same
Feeling love with touch of their hands
Hands I've wanted one more time
Lord, make it come true, my life will come anew
As I rock in this chair of loneliness

Viola B. Kilpatrick
Chandler, AZ

Hush Now, Baby

Hush now, baby, don't you even consider a sigh
Now that you're here, my life will be full when I die
Hush now, baby, don't you fret as to why the world's a mess
Despite the global despair, our moments are always the best

Shut your pretty eyes to the rampant bloodshed and unending war
Open them up for me to see better than anything I've seen before
Close your ears to the political excuses and those with agendas
If you can hear what I say and respond, oh, how tremendous

There are catastrophes and calamities that plague the Earth
But only great things have come since your long-awaited birth
Struggles now include terror, disease, and unemployment
Welcome, my angel, Sophia, the purest form of sheer enjoyment

Hush now, baby girl, there's no reason to cry today
A little sunshine and a breath will dry those tears away
Often life delivers things as unpredictable as the weather
My fluttering heartbeat stabilizes whenever we're together

Hush now, baby, let's focus on all that's good in the world
Release the tensions of infanthood, allow your fingers to uncurl
Just keep doing what you do best and show me that smile
I carry your love every inch, every foot, every single mile

Peter V. Lomp
Oakland Gardens, NY

257

The Passing

Out of the blue, the storm was sure.
Not a hint of rain, the air smelled pure.
Around the corner, there would be pain,
Life would never be the same again.

Gone was the picture he portrayed,
His perfect profile, no longer to stay.
He was here, happy, healthy, and fine
Then he was gone, body and mind.

He should have grown older,
His hair should have grayed,
He should have had wrinkles.
These were never made.

How do I justify loss of this kind?
How do I deal with this over time?
Where do I go to replace his joy?
Why does it hurt so, loss of this man-boy?

Together we came through a life of dismay,
A brother and sister showing each other the way.
Now I am one, my heart has been broken
For all of the words that will never be spoken.

Now he is gone, it still makes no sense
He is my rock and now emptiness.
With each day, I struggle to forget.
With each breath, I pray I never will.

Ronnie E. Macisco
Shelton, CT

I am currently living in Connecticut with my husband. I have recently been displaced
in my position as a financial advisor from Wachovia Bank. I am unemployed. I
have a daughter and two wonderful grandsons, ages twelve and eight. This poem
is my tribute to my brother, Jim, whom I lost unexpectedly. He and I shared a very
difficult childhood, and as a result, became closer than most siblings. When I lost
him, the pain was unbearable and so I turned to my writings to try to get through it.

Secret of Poetry

Poetry brings to mind the true
significance of life
Emotion of an experience long gone
a thought in memory
never forgotten held on

Frances A. Alicandri
Pittsburgh, PA

Untitled

We might save the Earth if we all
do our part and not keep polluting
our waters, our streams, our Earth, our planet
we all love so dearly love.
If we'd just look at our future, our land
where we'd be in twenty years or more
if we keep on disrespecting the life
we were meant to lead and believe that
it's nature, greenery that helps us lead
the life we want we want to lead and breathe.
If we just took a moment, a deep breath, a full gaze,
we'd realize it's all God's land, not ours,
it's His plan, not ours.

Cheryl Blindauer
Chicago, IL

Walk with Me

Walk with me this glorious day
Let me show you my caring way
Thoughts of love for you will come true
Walk with me, enjoy life's unending view

One day at a time, resounding love said
Until the day we unite and blissfully wed
Eternal love we may experience together
Walk with me in fair skies or stormy weather

No one can tell us the why or the how
Or when to walk in life as one, it could be now
Come share with me all the good and the bad
Walk with me in times of happiness or being sad

We will watch the sunrise and the sunset
Giving God thanks, blessing the day we first met
Sharing life's greatest challenge, love, as one
Walk with me as we wait for life on Earth to be done

The Lord gave us the ability to think and to feel
Our words and our actions will ultimately reveal
Endless love and hardships, all of life's reality
Walk with me, share true love for all eternity

Lucia A. Weisman
Long Beach, CA

Faded Blue Lighthouse

There you stand
Seated upon land
Faded blue lighthouse
Dated shades of pale blue
Faded shades of gray
Perched upon a rocky hill,
Standing still
Shadows of time
Days of yesterdays
Gone!
Time stopped in its tracks
Days faded away
Silently tiptoeing afar
Enormous white-capped waves rolling in
Rolling, dancing ashore
Waves breaking forevermore
Seashells washed up to gray faded door
Come tapping at your door
Seashells singing their song
Alive once more!

Donna M. Dziadul
Southport, CT

The Shrine at 161st and Jerome

It was a Sunday in June of 1956
My dad said we had to wear our best and shine
We were leaving for 161st and Jerome
It was my first trip to the shrine

It was built they say by a man named George
Like the guy they called Babe legends would play
Giants of blue in winter would roam
And the best of pugilists would have their day

Entering Gate 4 to a field so green
My stomach was nervous and my heart beat wild
As throngs of people arrive on the scene
I glanced at my father and he gave me a smile

There were times when many
Would join a pope to pray and
Scores would be jubilant
As musicians would play

My children and grandson have followed me there
Sharing my memories at 161st and Jerome
All that is left there now is a pile of stone
But across the street another generation will make
Memories of their own.

Robert W. Sellazzo
Cortlandt Manor, NY

Letter

Your letter of yesterday I took, fleeing home to unknown.
It was cold and dark before the dawn,
But carrying it like light, like talisman,
I could see the way. I know it said:
"I see you soon; if not tomorrow, the sixth of June."
I read and read at night and at noon,
And waited, waited at all crossroads to see you soon.
Many times, sun brought the June, and cold December came again.
Now, over the paper, yellow and old
Over tender words, and writing strong and bold,
Appeared your face of long ago,
Young and handsome, the way I know.
But my tears turned it into a salty sea,
I saw the ships overturning
And going down without a trace.
No one came home that night,
And only few crossed to the other side.
After fifty years, I still have your letter.
Where are you?

Emily Poulik
Panama City Beach, FL

When I came to this beautiful land, I knew only one word—okay. I thought it was odd that the first book I got was the John Keats Oxford Edition, 1910. I memorized "La Belle Dame Sans Merci," and my American friends had a big laugh when I proudly recited it. The second poem I learned by heart was Edgar Allan Poe's poem, "Annabel Lee;" it made me cry. It was my way of learning the American language. I have two dear daughters to whom I write and recite my poetry.

The Sly Controllers

Pelosi and Reid, the Dems and Obama too
Are all out to get us, that's me and you.
They hide in the night, in secret they plan
To plunder and control every woman and man.

They push, shove, and turn up the heat,
Award huge bribes, they won't be beat.
They give themselves a raise, a jet or two,
And wonderful health care that's not for me and you.

Seniors and veterans are a nuisance and a pain,
They hope we'll go away and none remain.
Murder, they wrote as they kill babies in the womb
To throw them into a garbage can tomb.

This is our government, and yes, you need to fear
As the destruction of our country goes into full gear.
They ignore the Constitution and do it their way,
ACORN, Mao, and Marxists are good, they say.

If you love your country, it's time to take a stand,
Wake up, be aware, scream, yell, and demand.
Hold onto your freedom, be willing to fight,
Or our future will be a long, dark night.

Stella A. Richardson
Sequim, WA

You Must

You must rejoice to the Lord.
Lift your voices high while you sing to the Lord.
Touch His Soul and Spirit from your voice.
You must praise Him.
Show the Lord how much you care.
You must pray to Him.
Ask Him what you can do for Him.
There is so much that He has blessed us with.
He has touched our hearts very much.
To show the Lord that the love we have for Him
You must dance to the Lord
To celebrate with the Lord, which is wonderful.
He was shown us the new meaning of life.
The affection that He was given us.
Just show the Lord what you can do for Him.

Brenda Wilsea
Anchorage, Ak

The Rose

How beautiful blooms the bright reddish rose,
Though stems be thorny, the buds stay tender.
The full blown flower inspires innate prose.

The rose means love to the female gender,
It remains the world's treasured flower,
And is most apt from a secret sender.

From it a young man receives love power
When he gives the maid a flower so fresh,
Hand-picked from a beautiful rose bower.

Now, maid and man and rose and love all mesh.

Louise F. Stirling
Leeds, UT

Hold on Tight

Your hands are really shaking something awful
as you light up your last cigarette.
How long have you been sitting in the darkness
can you not remember or do you forget.
How about the bottle of whiskey that is on the table.
does it make you feel better or just make you unable?
You know you are getting hard to be with
and you're crying every time you turn around.
You wonder why you cannot pick you head up
from off of the ground.
Everybody looks at you like they don't speak your language
and you are living at the bottom of a well.
You have swallowed all of you terrible dark secrets
that you could never tell.
You aught to get yourself together
but you cannot bare to walk outside the door.
No you cannot even bare to look into the mirror anymore.
As all your worries crawl all around your clothes.
How long will you sit in the darkness only heaven knows?
Don't ever give up my baby and don't turn out the light.
I am on my way to help you just hold on tight.

John C. Farmer
Williamston, SC

My Feathered Friends

It's wintertime with frost on the trees
From my window I see the chickadees

Every year they show up when the summer ends
To me, they're my little feathered friends

The feeders swing from the old ash tree
Full of seeds and goodies that they'll soon see

The sparrows are there, blackbirds and wrens
And now the feeding frenzy begins

If they could talk, what would they say
Thanks for breakfast on this cold winter's day
Now winter is gone and spring begins
The chickadees leave, the robins move in

Next winter, cabin fever will come again
I'll sit at my window and then begin

To rename all my new little
Feathered friends.

John B. Asher
Battle Mountain, NV

I live in northeastern Nevada, where it snows every winter. While having a coffee and brandy one morning, I noticed the birds coming to the feeders, and that is how this poem came about. I hope it will be enjoyed.

Friends Are the Flowers That Bloom in Life's Garden

Friends to me are precious and dear,
And become more so with each passing year
When I have days I feel down,
I give them a call and they come around.

They're always there to make things right,
And it makes my life feel much more bright
They seem to know just what to say
To brighten up my dreary day.

Be thankful for each friend you make,
Because they'll be there for all time's sake
Be sure to thank them along the way
For helping you make it through each day.

So to all my friends who have help me through,
I want to send thanks from me to you.

Delores J. Garbrick
Zephyrhills, FL

I'm Just Me

I still have morning cups of coffee
I don't cook eggs and bacon anymore
Since you're not here, I just snack on the go
I don't like mornings, I hate the nights even more
But I have to get to sleep, so I'll have to face the bed alone
I've been crying all night long since you've been gone
I need to find my way back to tour arms
I don't try to stand on my own
These things happened to other people I've known
But I can't believe what's happening to me
They tell me, things will get better, just wait and see
But I'm not other people, I don't have their strength
I don't know their secrets I just know I'm weak
You are my weakness, you're my strength
You are the reason I stay awake
And you're the reason I dream
No, I'm not like other people,
I'm just me.

Sarah F. Boykins
Tampa, FL

Never Alone

Lifting my heart to Heaven above
Thinking of God on His throne
I feel His presence ever so near
And I know that I'm not alone

Speaking His name in a tone of love
He answers, "I am here"
This presence I'll cherish above all Earth's wealth
And forever I'll hold it dear

My prayer today is that God above
Always will answer my voice
With His presence forever to fill me with love
Then forever I'll always rejoice.

Hazel B. Belk
Kannapolis, NC

Deliverance

In the coming of the brightening dawn
I knew I could no longer be his pawn
Somehow I had to right the terrible wrong
And learn to live the music in the song.

All the bright promises were in dreams
I could no longer survive the schemes
Even in sleep, I confronted the fears
The laughter did not outweigh the tears.

As my mind was clearing from the mist
I felt like life had cast me adrift
Escape the only avenue from this city
The only true companion was my kitty.

I know not what fog I floated within
But I had to become a fighter to win
His cruelty and torture were through
I took a step, opened the window, and flew.

Deborah M. Reimann
Gig Harbor, WA

The Smile

It was just an ordinary smile,
if there is such a thing,
but it seemed much more to me
coming from Martin Luther King.
His smile told a story of the places he had been,
and it seemed to lift the burdens of what I was doing then.

In a moment, he was gone, swept up by the crowd
to inspire a class of graduates,
who cheered him long and loud.

But no cheers can fathom the calm quiet on his face,
for with it was carried the hope of the Human Race.
I never will forget that smile,
nor can it be erased.
It gives me hope and courage for a people and a race.

William C. Evans
Versailles, KY

Then and Now

A lifetime ago, my heart dreamed of kisses in the moonlight
And days filled with the laughter of children.
My dreams were silenced. I thought forever.
Because of you, my heart dreams again.
These dreams are not those of my youth.
Now I dream of moonlight kisses
And sunlit hours filled with you.

Norma E. Taylor
St Louis, MO

I was born in December 1940 in Crawford County, Missouri to Earl and Ruth Thomas. I attended three one-room schoolhouses up through the sixth grade. I graduated from Steelville Elementary school in 1954 and moved to St. Louis in 1955, where I graduated from Central High School in 1958. I will be retiring this spring from my position as graduate coordinator in the chemistry department at Washington University for the last nineteen years. I have been writing poetry since I was thirteen years old. I have only shared my writings with a few select friends until a classmate I met at a recent high school reunion encouraged me to enter my writing into poetry contests.

Just Give Me the Necessities

I've seen so many people who worship the dollar
They feel it's really important to have more than their friends,
Buying everything new that comes on the market
Dressing their kids in the newest trends.

These people are so busy buying and spending,
Always taking the simple things in life for granted,
Never having the time to spend with loved ones,
Nor smelling the roses that have been planted.

Material things have no feelings
They can't hug you or say "I love you,"
Nor can they comfort you when you're sick,
Dry your tears when you're feeling lonely and blue.

Self-esteem, self-worth and inner peace of mind
Are much more important to me than material things.
It's always possible to lose material things
But you'll never lose the happiness that peace of mind brings.

I've never needed a lot of material things to make me happy,
Just give me a roof over my head and plenty to eat,
Good health, good friends, and someone to love me;
To me, that's a life can't be beat.

Edna M. Coon
Germantown, OH

Busy Sidewalks

Our biggest problem in eighteen-eighty
Is the growth of horse manure in our biggest cities!
Some of the brightest merchant
Minds and eastern politicians surmise
That a breed of faster horses, if produced,
Would then allow all to see to our
Dealings throughout town in quicker fashion
And with less wasted time. Too, this would permit
Men, beasts, and buggies to return to
Their liveries and then put down their loads.

Now nineteen hundred arrives and mankind
Only stares at the birds above his plains.
Surely, if God wanted his children to
Fly, He would have endowed us with silver
Wings to soar high atop tall buildings,
O'er our darling snow-capped Rockies, even
Over the oceans! But of what aims? Trains,
Tricycles, and steamships appear to remain
The eternal means for movement. Oh,
How could, why shouldn't anything be more right?

It's already nineteen forty! Uncle Sam's
The only one who can spare us a dime!
Just ask Louis Armstrong how dry it's been!
Chickens lay, and cows give us cream—income
For rich bankers' wives to order from Wards
Fancy pink curtains for their front porches.
Sears and Roebuck share the Trib and tan from
Hammocks in Hawaii (unaware how
We use their catalogs!). President Roose-
Velt is Rudolph, the Red-Nosed Reindeer.

Groovy! Now it's nineteen sixty! Basil
Dearden will direct a film of fearless
Astronauts. They need men immune to wor-
Ry and the common cold to go to the
Moon. "Kennedy Elected President."

Enter twenty-ten, when we've been advised
The chief crisis is carbon! Late in
November, one monarch butterfly that,
By then, should have been at Mariposa,
Paused to observe the columbines and milkweeds,
Stopping off at Greeley to brood awhile,
How millions of years ago her ancestors
Spent their first winter in Houston,
A primeval journey long before hers;
As she muses, her wings suggest that there
Might not have been enough poison in this
Year's crop to fulfill the hopes she was count-
Ing on and make her change significant
It's likely too soon to know. Yet in Yel-
Lowstone, some sulfur springs summer hotter.

Jeffery Moser
Aurora, CO

Jeff Moser (1961-?) was born in South Dakota. His father was a farmer and his
mother was an elementary school teacher and principal. He studied at the University
of Minnesota in Minneapolis and completed a bachelor's degree in English at the
University of Denver, Colorado, in 2008. He is currently finishing his master's at
the University of Denver. "I feel I am, first, a student of literature; second, a visual
artist; and third, a creative writer. My poetry often focuses on religious themes,
history, and issues of politics, society, environment, experimentation, and the human
condition." This poem encompasses these themes. In this poem, particularly raised
are questions of what is lasting and why and how?

Where Did Time Go?

My children were once two small boys
Who played with color crayons and toys.
They grew older and it was off to school,
It was time to learn the golden rule.
Time went on, the years flew by,
Now it was time for junior high.
Their interests changed, there are no more toys.
They chased the girls now, like other boys.
Sports, music, and Boy Scouts too,
There were girlfriends and jobs after school.

Where did the time go, I want to know
Just where on Earth did my babies go?

They finished high school, they both say
We will finally graduate and be on our way.
They are grown men and out of school
We often wondered what they will do.
My sons are now two married men
With lives of their own, and I ask,

Where did the time go, I want to know
Just where on Earth did my babies go?

They have their own lives and have moved away.
I knew the time would come, they would not stay.
I live alone now, but my family grew,
I now have two daughters and grandchildren, too.

Where did the time go, I want to know
Just where on Earth did my babies go?

Lorene A. Steelmon
Sun City, CA

Gramma

Faded flowers in a simple vase.
Faded quilt with hand-stitched seams.
Iron bedstead painted white.

Doctors call it a hopeless case.
She lies there in her silent dreams,
Nearer now to eternal night.

The devil will give up the chase.
Old preacher's face, believing, gleams,
His hand on hers to still the fright.

Her family now fills up the space
Around her bed until it seems
Their loving shines out, vivid bright.

I stand in awe to see her face,
And silently my shocked soul screams
In awe as life to light!

What others do her arms embrace,
Now gone from here to live her dreams?
What dawning follows now her night?

Charles D. Poole
Westminster, CA

In the deepest place of one's being, each person is a poet, living out the images that have their beginning in the mind. Pause and listen and share the silent songs of souls who pass near, whose words are here. In the sharing is joy. In the joy is peace.

Wine Vine

Wine vine, how delicious your glorious fruit!
It seems to nag my tasting zones! I loot
your bottled spirits for my own religion
of holy attitudes, to ride my pigeon

on wings of blackberries and ripe plum!
Oh . . . wait, my fingers grip with my thumb,
the tilted glass to trickle out a fainted song!
I cannot last the more of cycles long!

Drip, you hysterical wine vine, your mutilated
children of bloody glass of titillated
and breaking flavors of souls of your issue!
Ah . . . I sniff and eyes forsake the tissue.

But I cry for the gluttony to master my lips
to chew and lay on palate, disappearing grips
on licorice and dark chocolate! I follow
your last and fading trickle . . . I swallow!

Charles Edmunde Clary
Kelseyville, CA

Solution: Violence

Take a look at your god's plan,
does it include that gun in your hand?
Don't lose face, it's the only one you have,
for we stand with our backs to the water,
drowning in inches of humanity
while growing miles of insanity.

Will you fall on the day we are judged or stand as a judge?
These quiet riots marching on Capitol Hill
only shake the ground which you stomp.
Fear and tradition reigns from a throne
feeding the seed of revolution.

Is life over or is it just time to die?
Kill the man, silence the speech, erase the words,
but embrace the ideas to achieve a bleeding heart
from those who shout gently into the desolate air,
"It's not okay to think everything is all right."

Has this endless fight for control killed human compassion?
A sucker punch of reality in a blind world reveals wasted efforts
for a united world while persistent rebels of society
dream of better days to come tomorrow.

What did we do to deserve a violence like this?
Wash the stains of guilt and fear from our minds.
Each night I lay me to sleep, in routine
I pray to forget the troubles I've made,
start a new day in a new way among my brothers of progression.

Randy A. Stift
Irvine, CA

Let's Be to the Heavens

Sunshine in your eyes
and words on a paper
let's be to the Heavens
to be seen from the
world of the words
to Lord of Heavens
to you
Let's be to the Heavens
Let's be to the Heavens
Sky blue rain and dew
on the morning
Paper of ink to the
hand of words
Let's be to the Heavens
Let's be to the Heavens
Blue waters to the Earth of life
Hold the keys to live
Let's be to the Heavens
to grow
into the trueness
of life
Sunshine into the Earth
from Heavens
make it blessing of
us to have on our
lives to have
of want we can and want to have
Let's be to the heavens
Let's be to the heavens
to hold on your hands for holy blessings

Patricia Ann Belling
Wallace, MI

My Friend

I received a message from home today.
It said my dearest friend had passed away.
My heart filled with sadness and I began to cry,
As I started to remember the times gone by;
When we worked together, in the heat of the day
Knowing how much we cared without having to say.
I was always there for her, as she was for me,
We were as confident in our friendship as anyone could be.

Then one day, I decided to move away,
And goodbye to my friend was hard to say.
Although we always stayed in touch,
I thought of her every day, and missed her so much.
Then my heart lifted when I stopped to think;
Someday, we will be together again, as quick as a wink.
We will stroll for all eternity, hand in hand,
On streets of gold in the promised land.

Jo Ann L. Hunter
Huntingburg, IN

My Child

My child, my child, God's crying out to you—
You're in my hands—I've chosen a few.

In suffering we grow and become strong,
To Him forever we cherish and belong.

Take comfort, He is by your side,
To heal, to guide, and in your heart abide.

Your suffering will not be in vain,
Others you'll help and feel their pain.

Take care and know that God is in charge,
In Him place your burdens, no matter how large.

A great plan for your life He does hold,
He wants you to trust and be bold.

Count your blessings, more than a few,
Better days are coming, so don't be blue.

Greatness starts and comes from within,
With God on your side, you will win.

You are not alone, He will not part,
You are special, and loved from the heart!

Marshelle G. Carberry
Fresno, CA

The Spirit of Christmas

The season's upon us, it's that time of year
To give of good tidings and spread lots of cheer.
The stockings are hung, the tinsel is bright,
The fire is crackling so warm through the night.
There's cookies and candy and all sorts of food,
The eggnog and fruitcake create the right mood.
The tree is assembled with stars and bright lights,
All the colors aglow, what a beautiful sight.
Our families all gather to share in the feast
Of laughter and love, of joy and of peace.
The blessings are counted and thanks be to God.
For all of His mercy, to Him we applaud.
So sing and rejoice, keep the spirit of love,
For Christmas is sent as a gift from above.

Renay L. Ivens
Fairfax, VT

How Much Longer?

Russ was my father-in-law, but he was more like my father.
He was kind, generous, loving, and at the end,
his trust in me was like no other, and that was the
greatest feeling of all.
Story telling was his passion,
and he was the master even at the ripe old age of eighty-eight.
From taking the mule to town on a snowy Iowa morning
or making soap with his mom, even making homemade
molasses, he remembered it all.
His childhood sweetheart got the best deal—
a navy man, an implement business, five kids,
and sixty-seven years of marital bliss.
Sometimes, bad times can turn into good times,
blessed times, like when I got laid off and the house
across the street foreclosed, Russ and his sweetheart moved in.
His kidneys started to fail, so dialysis
became a dreaded part of our lives.
Three times a week, I would take him and pick him up
with a glass of sweet tea to drink,
which he called "southern joy."
He lost his strength in the last few weeks
and his wife would call when he fell out of bed
or couldn't get up from his chair,
but not once did he complain while lying on that floor,
only a joke to make us laugh while we picked him up.
He would always ask, "How much longer can this last?"
That was answered on December 1, 2008.
Two full years with him were a blessing indeed.
What a man, what a father, what a friend.

Richard W. Pittman
Rock Hill, SC

You Gave Me

Restore my soul
That I will see
The blood You
Shed for me.

You gave me strength
When I was weak
You gave me hope
When I had none.

You gave me a passion
For people to live
A life for You
When they have none.

You gave me faith
That I will see
My Savior's love
Who died for you and me.

Betty R. Patterson
Goshen, IN

Endearing Earth

Rose so fair I tend your bloom
tracing the petals now opening

I hum a breath to praise your beauty
and in reverie am wondering

The Earth too soon is growing old
for Man forsakes his promise

Spurn freshness of air and sparkle of water
I fear the dread upon us

The north sky bares a blazing sun
that scorches the sea below

Trees cry silent pitiful tears
and the grass has lost its glow

An angry sun carves rugged fissures
to blemish the dear Earth's crust

Sudden is a morning haze
and the rocks have turned to dust

Rose so fair I sense your pleading
in hope your prayer is felt

Will Man take a stand before
the hand of the universe is dealt

Hold in your heart to love the Earth
since our future may be dim

Love the Earth as God loves it
Surely it is precious to Him

Marilyn Maddalone
Acra, NY

My Big Bro

You came into my life back in 1953,
I was little sis to you, you were big bro to me.
From the very beginning, we had a strong start,
We were inseparable; we were never apart.
As we became older and shared what we knew,
We learned much from each other while each of us grew.
And even though we argued as brothers and sisters do,
We had a special bond; hugs for me, kisses for you.
You were my stability and of you I was so proud,
Through life's setbacks, I just want to scream out loud . . .
"You're my big bro, I'm your little sis,
Give me a hug, and I'll give you a big kiss!"
You're now in Heaven, I am here trying not to cry,
God has called you home, I know the true reason why.
It was your special time, you were only fifty years old,
For God had a plan to see streets of glorious gold!
Say hi to our family, for you are with them today,
Give them a hug from me; listen, I just want to say . . .
Dave, please know I love you; you, I will truly miss,
You're my big bro, I'm your little sis!

Nancy K. Wilson
Ellettsville, IN

Poetry has always been a part of my life and the words come from my heart. It expresses my innermost thoughts when normal words cannot be found. This poem is no exception. My brother passed away on January 17, 2001 at the young age of fifty years old. This poem was written in the early morning the day of his funeral.

God Is in My Heart

God is in my heart, He guides my soul
though the gardens of peace, passing by
the forbidden fruits of love to the waterfalls of
happiness, laying in the grass of joy, breathing
in the air of health; the caring animals surrounding
the meadows of comfort and the trees of life.
A companion by my side with the sunlight
lit up bright and flowers blooming with delight.
Walking by the riverside, looking from eye to eye,
my heart filled with laughter, no tears of hate,
just a smile to pass around.
Living in the cave with the bears to keep us warm,
laying in a bed of leaves with the sounds
of crickets putting us to sleep; with rain pouring on
the ground and a fire roaring nearby,
I know I am safe with you by my side.
No matter what spells I may fall upon,
I'll always know there's a path planned for me.
I will not let evil get in the way,
I will not let temptation stand in my way,
I will live a straight and narrow life
because God will always be in my heart.

Steven D. Dawes
Henderson, NV

A Special Artist

God must be a special artist
To paint the world in so many different hues
To blend in all the colors
Of the reds, yellows, and blues.
The mountains and the seashores
All perfect in the ways
The burnt red, golden autumn leaves
The cool, fresh spring days.
He took his brush with special care
And painted the sky blue.
Yes, He painted the world so beautiful
Just for me and you.

Marilyn Love
E. Bernstadt, KY

I have found in this life that there is nothing too small or too great not to be considered. Love thy neighbor would fix most, if not all, of the world's problems. As for my poetry, I cannot do anything without the Lord. After all, He is the author and finisher of all words.

The Price of Freedom

"A time for peace and a time for war,"
The good book rings this chime.
The issue is not the right to fight.
The fight is over the time.

The paradox is that the cons condone
Man's cruelty, death, and hate,
While the pros promote
Man's love and freedom as being his fate.

Patricia M. Wells
Mt. Vernon, IL

My goal when writing a poem or essay is to present the truth so simply and clearly that no one can refute it. The truth shall indeed set us all free. My favorite author is Rudyard Kipling and my favorite poem is Kipling's "If." My favorite book is the King James Version of the Judeo-Christian Bible.

Untitled

This is such a cloudy day,
It seems the world has gone astray.
You hear of such misery of souls,
The pain and suffering untold
Of lives torn to no repairs,
Of people of the world who care.

You pray that God somewhere will hear,
And send angels down to calm their fears.
You hope and pray with them all.
You hear the generations that will fall,
No more to carry on the life
As it was before the strife.

Oh, dear God, please hear their call,
And catch them all as they fall.
They feel as if it's a never again life,
But they should know God is forever in might.

Dorothy Feldner
Philadelphia, PA

The Incredible Door

Jesus' name is the key to unlock the door
To a heavenly relationship you never knew before
When you call Jesus' name your situation will change
You have tried everything else that has left you in pain
Get filled with the Holy Spirit He will give you the heart to obey
The Lord of true life wants to bless you in every way

Andrea K. Murrell
Ft. Washington, MD

The Pencil

Why do they pick on me, put
me in a drawer?

Sometimes I stay out and I'm used,
then I'm thrown away. I'm important, too.
I have a name and can help people.

Please don't use me up and throw me away.
I love to be held and used to help people.

I'm only a pencil, but also a friend.
What can we write today?

Barbara S. Freeman
Charlotte, NC

Candle in the Corner

I'm just a candle in the corner, so tiny and so small.
No one really knows me, and no one comes to call.
Forgotten by some, but not by all.
Pushed aside by fear and fright,
I still shine brightly, morning till night.
My flame will not flicker nor be snuffed out by sin.
I'm just a candle in the corner shining brightly for Him.

Ellen A. Gaskey-Berryman
VA Beach, VA

I was inspired by a radio program I was listening to on my way to work. "You can be as small as a candle or as big as a lighthouse to be a beacon for God." Through Him, all things are possible.

Mountains High

Winding roads and mountains high
Where eagles soar to touch the sky

Lakes full of turtles and trout
Wild turkeys are trotting about

Squirrels are hiding in the colorful trees
Through the air comes the mountain breeze

It's so beautiful in the country
As far as one can see
Where you always run wild and free

Bobbi J. Hager
Ozark, AL

Wondering

Life is an ember!
A glowworm of night,
Burning, churning,
An enigma in flight!

Breath is its keeper—
Love is its light!

Life is a firefly in flight!

Miona Hyde-Sullivan
Oklahoma City, OK

Marriage

What does a marriage need a marriage to make
A license and a ritual does not a marriage make
Lust and passion will not a marriage make
These are but a base upon which to build for a marriage to make
Love and commitment are steps a marriage must take
Communication when troubles arise as they will a marriage must take
Honor and honesty will surely help a marriage to make
Love must grow and chores be shared a marriage to make
Forgive and forget a need for a marriage to make
All this and more plus God's blessing is a need
To make a marriage succeed

John W. Young
Folsom, CA

Finding Well-Being

When the sun sets over an expanse of water,
A peaceful sense of well-being descends.
As the water ebbs and flows,
The cares of the day seem less foreboding,
And tomorrow will bring a new day of hope,
Accompanied by the rays of the sun to warm the soul.

Janet L. Routson
Amarillo, TX

Perseverance

The wind whispers
Branches flow in graceful dance
Demonstrating strength and agility.
Life is like the wind,
Gentle breezes . . . fierce winds . . . quiet calm.
Respond as the trees
Gracefully swaying
Bending, yet not breaking,
Withstanding the forces.
It is in bending
We shall not break.
As the wind subsides,
All is calm.

Donna L. Choudhry
Blenheim, NJ

The Mother That I Wish Were Mine

The mother that I wish were mine I truly hold dear,
She knows just what to say to calm my fears.
She knows just what to say when I feel I can't go on,
The mother I hold dear makes me feel like I belong.

The mother I wish were mine is a woman of strength,
When I need compassion, she really goes the length.
The mother that's so dear is in fact not mine at all,
But she is always there to catch me when I fall.

The mother that I wish were mine is my inner light,
When life seems dim, she's there to make it bright.
Tears of sadness, I try so hard to resist,
Because I wonder if she really knows that I exist.

My heart feels so much like it wants to bleed,
I wish I knew if her words were true indeed.
I pray for my soul to be at peace in time,
I cry for the mother that I wish were mine.

Leslie V. Puckett
Newport News, VA

A Song in My Heart

There's a song in my heart, I can hear it so clear,
it's the one that I sing with the thought of you here.
I can take you to places inside of my soul
that will reach you and teach you, your heart I can hold.
This journey begins with the thought of your touch,
your loving embraces, your kisses so much.
Every word like a whisper, a melody of time,
playing over and over again in my mind.
There's a song in my heart and I'm holding it dear
for the days and the nights that you're no longer here.
It will serve as a memory, so loving and true,
in those days that were yesterday for me and for you.
The passion embedded so deep in my heart,
with laughter and friendship, our lives from the start.
There's a song in my heart, I can sing it to you,
it's the same one we sing, and you know it, too.
And whenever our lives are over and done,
may you always remember that you were the one
that brought me from sadness to joy and content,
and I'll cherish each moment and never forget.
There's a song in my heart, there inside it will stay,
for precious are feelings no one can take away.
I will nurture and savor all my love that's for you,
and for all of the days and the nights we're apart,
it won't even matter, 'cause you're the song in my heart.

Annette F. Jusino
Roseboom, NY

The Loss of a Father

What is a father?
I do not know!
I haven't had one
from so long ago.

Why did he leave?
He did not say.
Didn't he love me?
I don't know to this day.

Would things be different
all those days long gone
if I never were
if I'd never been born?
I hold it inside
all the hurt and the pain
from the rejection I feel
from one man's game.

What will it take
to know and to feel
all the love of a father
that's true and so real?

Carol A. Setzer
Baldwinsville, NY

Can I Squeeze in Here?

Can I squeeze in here?
I'm quiet and won't take up much space
I've given my seat to too many things
and now I find myself displaced

I gave up my seat to love once
just packed up and moved away
I thought he was cute
and would make a good friend
I didn't know that he'd turn out to be an ofay

I gave up my seat to my daughter
to allow her to be
We don't understand each other now
and again, in the end, it's just me

I know that I could sit by myself
and there are lots of good shows on TV
but at this time, I would like to sit somewhere
not just in time and in me

Roeethyll Lunn
Dudley, NC

301

Whitewashed Cupboards

Dirty dishes in the white basin sink
White frilly curtains framing the dirty window
Screened door that needed to be washed
Wallpaper peeling from the walls of the kitchen

But the whitewashed cupboards that held
White porcelain dishes and bowls and cups
With a pull-out white panel for baking
And breadmaking was spotlessly clean

Victoria A. Borgerding
Westerville, OH

America for Me

America for me
it's my land of liberty
where I long to be
In the land of freedom
there's power in the air
and sunlight in the sky
The past is a lesson for
the present to make the future free
We love our land for what she is
and what she needs to stay
Oh, it's home, land of the free.

Wardell M. Brown
Las Vegas, NV

Patchwork Soul

My life is as the pieces of a patchwork quilt,
Anger, joy, and sorrow interlaced with guilt.
Mediocrity comprising its center band,
With small victory squares sewn in carefully by hand.
Stitches reinforcing the outer edge of each square
As protection against unraveling and becoming threadbare.
In crisis, the stitching pulls taut, but does not break,
And settles back unwrinkled in each trauma's wake.
Each piece of anguish, just as thoroughly sewn
As those lovingly stitched in a happier tone.
Unpredictably interspersed here and there,
You'll find an inexplicable spontaneity square,
Which gives the design a hint of something unexpected,
Though quite often, it's gazed upon undetected.
My patchwork quilt grows more voluminous every year,
And I hope when the final stitch is in place, I won't fear
That I've inadvertently left an essential piece out
To leave my patchwork spirit riddled with regret and doubt.

Sheryl D. Gleason
Pinellas Park, FL

Just Another Day in Paradise

I'm staying here in this wonderful place,
it came as quite a surprise.
I didn't know I would break my leg.
Rehab's such a paradise.
The doctors, they have put me here
because they are oh, so wise.
The meals are delivered right to me,
fixed just to tantalize.
My brace is a lovely thing to see,
and the gowns, they are just my size.
The bed I sleep in, has buttons galore.
It goes down when I press it to rise.
There are so many things to do here,
more than you'd realize.
If you wheel yourself around the place,
you'll meet up with most of the guys.
The rehab room is a really nice room,
with a view that will please the eyes.
If you follow the tips that your therapist gives,
good health will be your prize,
The treatment that you receive here
is nothing to despise,
and all the roomies have such fun.
Just another day in paradise.

Sharon E. Olmos
Huntington Beach, CA

My Mama's Hands

They are loving and kind,
Now old, thin, and blue-lined.
They cleaned the house and cooked the meals,
Ironed the clothes and paid the bills.
Buttons and hems they are still able to sew,
And beautiful handwriting from those fingers flows.
Although her hands are now rough and worn,
They held me lovingly when I was born.
Every night with folded hands, they taught me how to pray,
To ask God to keep me safe throughout the coming day.
They disciplined me when I was bad,
But gave me a hug when I was sad.
Mama's hands are not strong like they used to be,
But they have always been there to hold and protect me.

Patricia J. Burney
Marietta, GA

See If You Can Guess What I Am

See if you can guess what I am.
I am yellow and fuzzy when I am just a baby.
I like to take naps in the warm sun.
I waddle when I walk and run.

See if you can guess what I am.
I like to eat corn and sneak up on bugs.
I have funny little webbed feet,
And a bill for snatching up things.

See if you can guess what I am.
I like to go swimming
And diving in nice cool water.
I flap my wings and quack when I get excited.

See if you can guess what I am.
I am a duck, my darling child,
And those are the things I do.

Adrienne R. Phaup
Amherst, VA

Lost

Deserted illusions haunt my troubled vision
As I gaze into the twisted glass
Naked trees stand alone
Empty skeletons of the past
The dark snow softly whispers
A song I cannot hear
Forgiven are the words
That remember the meaning
Of my very existence
Behind the walls I call my own
I cannot see the beauty past
Of shining armor and red roses
Lost is the way to the path beyond
The shattered steps still linger at my feet
Shadows dance through the gateway
In the depths of my mind
How long ago did time pass by
Without knocking on my window
Leaving but an empty sheet
Of forever and no more?
Still yearning for the season change
And maybe, just in time
A single little butterfly
May grant me
Another life. . . .

Sander Rinzema
Nashua, NH

Purple Dreams

The front gates before me as I stand in awe,
saying goodbye was the only flaw.
I will never again gaze upon the great tower,
the fountain court and smell the sweet rain shower.
The once grand staircase, now dilapidated and old,
boasts royalty dressed in jewels and gold.
As I behold the grounds of Bowling Green,
its majestic views can only be seen.
Under purple skies, she stands yet so tall,
with crumbled stone walls from many a fall.
In all her glory, she's still my dream,
as is in Camelot, life was only a scheme.
To say farewell, my castle of dreams,
where fantasies entwined my mind, so it seems.
I will always remember these magical times,
and yet relive with all its medieval crimes.
Today, the crowd of visitors, such a hassle,
as I turned and said, "Goodbye, Raglan Castle."

Jamie R. Mallinson
Zanesville, OH

Walking on Knives

Crooked legs, wasted . . . no place to go.
Unremitting struggle . . . the knife walk.
No rest. No mercy.
The promise of relief rides the wind and
Is swept away solemnly into the shadows.
Barbed wire tears and saws crimson grooves.
The chalk mountains with deep copper rivulets.
Rebecca, where can you go? Life is closed and cloudy,
And you so young and promising, with your warm
Dark eyes so penetratingly sad and distant.
Repose has no place.
Motionless forms look at despair
And have no answer.
Grinding grit of bone, lost dreams.
A medicine haze is a tricky life,
But walking on knives with no place to go is no life at all.

Linda C. Williams-Avila
Hercules, CA

Remember Me

Remember me in this you see,
And in this world, I may not be.
Remember the grave is not my bed,
I'll keep on living, I won't be dead.
I'll be with Jesus in Heaven above,
Where all is peace, joy and love.
So when you have a thought of me,
Remember, I'm not dead, I'm in eternity,
And you can see me again one day
If you'll accept Jesus and His way.
There are so many investments in Heaven for me,
A husband, parents, and others to see.
You see, you can stroll for miles and miles
And see many faces with great big smiles.
No tears, no sadness, no sickness no more,
Just loved ones and friends and saints of yore,
But the sweetest thing is to look in the face
Of the one who saved you by His amazing grace!
I know I won't feel worthy to bow at His feet,
But when He calls me home, my life He'll complete.
Completely with Jesus, I'll ever abide,
No devil to tempt me or draw me aside.
You see, I loved you while I was here,
You all were so precious and very dear,
But now that I'm gone and can't be with you,
Remember the precious times that we went through.
So many good memories to last till I meet you there
Yonder in Heaven, where all things are so fair!
I'll meet you there one day so sweet,
Just look for me at Jesus' feet!

Merle D. Bell
Cairo, GA

Pillars of Cloud and Fire

Why bow our heads to offer prayers?
See how the humanists toss theirs
And laugh at God in scorn.
Technology has power to bless
Without the crutch of righteousness
In turning night to morn.

If man's perfection we would find,
Our faith must be in all mankind,
And all men must be free.
We must abandon faith in God.
We must no more be overawed
By things we cannot see.

A global village, not a creed,
Will meet our children's every need—
One world, our sole desire.
If not from Heaven, then from Hell,
Shall men see Man's perfection well—
Pillars of cloud and fire?

James E. Irwin
Beaver, PA

Proud men reject the Pillar of Cloud and Fire who leads the humble from Mt. Sinai to Mt. Calvary. They reject the Law, which convicts them of sin and death. The proud will miss the grace of the cross and the joy of resurrection in Jesus Christ. Proud men will trust only in man-made pillars of cloud and flame produced by prideful technology. They will follow where these pillars lead.

I Live For

I live for
To right the wrongs
Of all the bad things
I have done
I live for
A world of peace
So we all can
Be free
In a world full of pain and sacrifice
We must try
To hold on to
The better things in life
Too much time wasted
On what we can get
Why can't we see
That life is a gift
I live for her loving
I live for peace
For you and me
I live
For the moment
We can all
Be free

Tyrone U. Jamerson
Omaha, NE

Easier to Breathe

Finally
It's easier to breathe
No more pain
My heart is at ease
No more tears
From all your lies
The pressure is gone
Now I rise
High in the sky
Alongside the birds
No more excuses
My voice is heard
So many memories
I can throw away
And never look back
At those suffocating days
I am stronger
More in control
You don't own me
Or my soul
Finally
It's easier to breathe
No more pain
My heart is at ease

Rachel M. Mazzella
Wellsburg, WV

The Friendship I Have with the Lord

I am walking around Chandler Park knowing
this wonderful and unique Spirit will protect
and bless me on a daily basis. I notice He is
getting on and off the two super-sized water
slides and wave pools around numerous kids,
teenagers, and adults while I am strolling by them.
This Spirit has shown and lectured me on various things.
He is everything to me.
I stroll by the golf course, noticing the golfers
with smiles on their faces, knowing that He is
in their life as they are playing golf with one another.
While recalling what I have shared
with this Spirit, I begin to think He is
awesome, well-built, and understanding
toward me. I am so thankful, cheerful, and
happy to have a long relationship with this
Spirit. The love and care we have for one
another will never change. I am also proud to
have Him in my life as I stroll around the park.
As I look up at Him, I know God is watching over me.

Kelli L. Thomas
Detroit, MI

Untitled

The ocean waves roll in slowly
Onlookers wait, anticipating, watching
The blue wall grows bigger, stronger
One story, two stories and higher
Each drop of water, a vital part of its life
As it approaches the beach, it roars with anger
The white tops flaring up high
Waiting to come down
The final movement in slow motion
Plenty of time to move out of the way or dive beneath
But paralyzed, no movement occurs
Until the wall of ocean water crashes down
Like thunder booming in the sky
Disturbing and forever changing the sand which it has hit
The ocean waves roll in slowly
But last only an instant
To leave change behind forever

Kelly J. Saunders
Reading, MA

Beautiful Redbuds

As you go through life's long highway
From your cradle to your grave
You shall never see a more beautiful sight
Than in the spring when the redbuds and the dogwood are in bloom
When my life on this Earth is over
And the Master calls me home
Wait till spring and scatter my ashes
In the grove at the bend of the river
Where the redbuds and dogwood intertwine
'Cause only God could make this shrine

Louis W. Lotman
Luray, VA

Love

Love is a constant battle
You'll win and you'll lose
Never knowing who's true and who's fake
Until you find the one

Love is a constant battle
Never knowing when it will end
Once you find the one
The battle is done—you've won
Love is a constant battle

Devon H. McCroskey
Wilson, NC

Small Miracles

Such tiny but well formed fingers,
Ten toes and a rosebud mouth
Another miracle has been wrought
By God in his infinite wisdom
And I, with unspeakable pride,
Claim to have had, although small, a part.

Quickly growing, ever changing
This life becomes alive and real.
Giggles, feelings, constant chatter,
With a mind that devours
And a love without question.
What else could possibly matter?

When tears come, and they will,
A big hugs of understanding
Is the cure - so simplistic, you see.
Learning with diligence
Words quickly digested.
Were we quite so clever when only three?

As a flower buds and grows
Gently blooming before the world
So does the child giving beauty and joy too.
While I in my infinite wisdom
Know life's greatest pleasure is in hearing
The words, "Grandma, I love you."

Marilyn G. Field
Portsmouth, VA

The Master Plan

This Earth that was created
By God and all that's good
Has slowly been corrupted
By Man who has never understood
That to conquer is not always
The wisest path to choose
For in taking control from God
He destined only to always lose
The madness that seems so prevalent

In humankind today
Is manifested in their attempts
To lead our youth astray
One can only find contentment
When they're willing to understand
That God has already given
Our answers in His mighty master plan

The world is searching frantically
For something to bring the joy
The peace and the contentment—
To our hearts and minds and toil

The answer isn't wealth
Nor riches in this world
The answer is found in only God
Please welcome Him and His Holy Word.

Brenda J. Thomas
Frostburg, MD

Walk with God

I walk with God hand in hand
Just like I was a child again.
I walk with God through sunshine or rain
From every moment of every day.
He is my Savior, my Master, and friend.
He takes my hand and shelters me
In His most secret holding place.
He draws me near by His side,
And leads me to higher ground.
I walk with God hand in hand
Just like I was a child again.
He is my life and He loves you, too.
He will be your peace, and is a loving God.
Walk with Him.
Let Him be your guide.

Linda M. Hielen
Shenandoah, IA

The House Guest from Hell

She was the house guest from hell that barely cleaned her room!
She was afraid of the vacuum cleaner
and had a restraining order against her broom.
She was lazy and could not manage her bills
as well as her bank deposits.
She had loads of clothes and lots of shoes
and hid everything else in her closet.
Sometimes when I visited,
her cleaning ability would be quite pivotal.
She was a single lady and a house guest from hell
and to most, a very lazy individual.
She always told me that her dream is to one day become a cop.
When she would spill things on the floor, she would not wipe it up.
Some believe that she was clearly allergic to the mop.
Cooking was not of her vernacular,
burning was something that she did spectacular.
Being a tidy woman is not of her concern.
Fruit flies, roaches, mice, and rats,
she will most likely be one of those old ladies
with three dead husbands, some old jewelry,
a Social Security check, and a house full of cats.

Kimberly Boyd
Washington, D.C.

I love to entertain people with my storytelling abilities. I love to turn a frown upside down. I have a degree in happiness. I appreciate the opportunity to share my poetry. God bless you all!

Weakening

At times and days when there was light,
Where some could see, and others not.
Most of the thoughts were still straight,
But creed arose mightier than thought.

Those days were perfect days of light,
Yet some could see, and others not.
Heart whereas dim was held straight,
Strong beliefs unfolded the thought.

Centuries came and went with light,
Yet some could see, and others not.
The soul was thin, but dwelled straight,
Weaker than creeds eloped the thought.

Now sense bestows far tidy light,
Where fewer can see, and others not.
Faith grew twisted, no longer straight,
With devious creeds expires the thought.

Grace Vera y Aragon
Kensington, MD

Open My Eyes

Lord open my eyes
That I may see
The needs of others
Not as blessed as me

Open my ears
That I may hear
Your voice when You
Speak loud and clear

Give me a heart to love
A heart to understand
Most of all I ask of You
Love for my fellowman

Georgia Stallings
Hampton, VA

I'm a mother, grandmother, and great-grandmother. I've been writing poems off and on for many years. Writing is a gift from the Lord, and I'm blessed and grateful He has allowed me to do it.

What a Jurist

She is a brilliant jurist
She prosecutes
Your evidence she persecutes
She educates
She intimidates
She humiliates
She exclaims, watch my face!
That you must do with lightning haste
She does not negotiate
You're thinking she navigates
She is rough and tough
She drinks no broth
Her sentence is fair, abrupt, and rough
Her father's name is not Rudy
But I guess her mom's name is Trudy
No wonder her name is Judge Judy.

John J. King
Dorchester, MA

February Snowfall

Bright sun glances off branches
Layered in snow.
Squirrels dart up and down
Precipitating avalanches.
Without a sound,
Snow falls on snow.
The ground beneath
Sleeps in frost,
A sparkling throw
Insuring winter's slumber.
Snowflakes without number
Tick away the season.
Clock-less birds
Know the sunbeams
With their daily brightening
Dance toward spring.

Tasha S. Halpert
Grafton, MA

The Godly Woman

A godly woman's virtue is without measure;
If one is found, she is a boundless treasure.
She's a priceless woman of industrious mind,
Does work with her hands of many kinds.

She rises early for her family to care,
Then diligently works, their food to prepare.
She buys good land and plants the seed,
Thus providing for her family's need.

Her husband knows he can safely trust,
He feels no need to stray or lust.
Because of her works, her virtue, and fame
Her husband is blessed; all know of his name.

Strength and honor, this woman does wear,
Wisdom is her words, her kindness and care.
She opens her mouth with wisdom to speak,
Her household is cared for, there's plenty to eat.

Few there be who live such a life,
Shunning the pitfalls of contention and strife.
"God, who created, who rules from the heart,
Give us more godly women to shine like the stars!"

Mary S. Parker
Sanford, NC

Puzzle

My life is made up of pieces,
Pieces of a puzzle,
Pieces of all shapes, colors, sizes, sounds.
These are the pieces that make up my life
I don't yet know how they are all supposed to fit together
Nor do I know exactly what the picture of my life will be at the end.
Some of the pieces are still being created.
My wants, desires, dreams, aspirations
Are also part of my puzzle.
How do they fit into my picture?
My past, my family's legacy are a core feature of my picture too.
They were the first pieces,
The first colors, sounds, shape, sizes
That began to form the puzzle I call my life.
They will continue to move and shape my picture.
I want my picture, my puzzle, my life to be
Your picture, Your puzzle, Your life.
You created me. You have created all the pieces of my life.
Don't just show me how to put them together.
Be with me as I put them together.
Create my picture with me.
I want You to be the subject of my picture.
Mold the pieces of my life to be what You desire for me.
I want my life, my picture, my puzzle
To fit into Your puzzle, Your picture.
Give me the ears to hear You, the courage to follow, and
The eyes to see how You are putting my puzzle into Your puzzle.

Helena E. Foster Fabiano
Greensboro, NC

Mother, a Gem

When I thought of the gems of the world
And the value for which they stood,
I became aware of the greatest gem,
The gem of motherhood.

They have beauty and value rare,
Renowned throughout the land,
But all their beauty cannot compare
To a mother's helping hand.

She is a gem of beauty rare
Which I prize above all other.
There is no gem you can compare
To the gem of a godly mother.

When mother reaches the city above,
A city of gems and gold,
She will stand out in the eyes of God
As a gem of beauty untold.

William B. Riffe
Bradshaw, WV

Searching

Sometimes I'm a shelf on the wall,
with figures all facing forward
and artfully arranged.

But mostly I'm slanting a little,
loosening from the wall
and ready to crash
at any time.

Sarah L. McBurney
Waldorf, MD

A Love Poem

I wish I could tell you how much I care,
But words alone can't tell what's there.
I'm happy when you're near and sad when you're afar,
As I try so hard to be your forever shining star.
When you said, "I love you," I tingled inside,
And though I was happy, I started to cry.
I want your love for me to be free,
I want you to want to return to me.
I could never love another, nor ever do you wrong,
No one could ever come between a love so strong.
Believe me, it's true, and I don't mean maybe,
That I honestly do love my baby!

Betty Ann M. Gill
Graysville, AL

Shamrocks in the Mist

Long centuries past one small plant
Communicated words of love and change
Patrick upon Erin's shore descended
Plucked from emerald earth one so tiny
Small and windswept deepest green
Proud symbol of the Celtic isle did become
Message of three, the holy ones
Its leafy patterns gently reflect abiding faith
In migrant waves came to lands so new
Bringing the emblem green and true
Passing on the message the verdant land held dear
Vapor trails ties from there to here
From mossy banks and rolling hills
Tender plant of forest hue whispers, hush, be still.

Betty A. Taucher
Mentor, OH

Winter Solitude

The days blow cold.
The night winds howl.
Bleak are the trees.
All leaves blown about—
A sad time,
A reflective time,
So forlorn, the plants, the trees.

Tomorrow, the days will be bright and sunny,
The evenings starlit.
The ground wet with new fallen rain—
The trees will burst forth
With newfound energy.

Green leaves sprouting on weathered limbs,
Buds appearing on bushes.
Apple blossom time will bring redbuds, white blossoms.
Strength renewed—
An end to winter's solitude.

Linda J. Glicco
Katy, TX

Recognizing

It's the excitement of the unknown
That gives us the need to seek.
It's the thorn on the rose
That makes them so unique.
It's the star who stands alone
For which a wish is reserved.
It's the luck for who discovers
Why the clover is preserved.
It's knowing it won't last forever
That makes us want to savor.
It's the craving for attention
That messes with our behavior.
It's the unbelievable glimpse of hope
That encourages the endless chase.
It's the fabulously forbidden title
That gives the fruit its unforgettable taste.
It's the anxiety of not knowing
That makes us ignore directions.
It's recognizing the true beauty
For its remarkable imperfections!

Jarrett H. Nash
New Market, MD

Change

As light comes in the morning sky,
So does the light of Heaven pierce my soul.
I stand in the glory of transformation.
I revel in the quiet changing
Of darkness into light,
And it is all because of God's amazing grace.

William J. Bess
Bremo Bluff, VA

Homeless Hearts

We are the ones who can bring joy.
We can brighten your life with our love.
Our silly ways, our playfulness, our kindness, and loyalty.
Not all of us started out in life with a good home and kind hearts.
We know that if we're good that maybe we can be part of your life.
We don't give up hope that one day, we will be loved.
We never asked to be in our situation.
We dream that one day, we will have a family to call our own.
We come from all over, but end up in the same places.
We can tell the kindness of those who take us in help us find a home.
We are the ones who are lost and alone,
We are the ones who want to be loved.
We are the homeless hearts.

Amanda R. Taylor
Tulsa, OK

Finding Solutions

Having a problem finding the solution
The answer lies within

Living is like attending class
The past are lessons learned

A problem is the test
A test passed is a learned lesson

The solution depends on
The classes taken and the lessons learned

Solve the problem
The solution is already earned

What have you learned

Carol L. Sumner
Newberg, OR

She Stands Alone

One soul centuries old. She stands alone.
A warrior from the beginning. A leader among none.

Created from light, born of the dark.
Hair as golden as the new sun. Eyes as
black as the night sky. Skin as brown
as the earth. Slender of build, too delicate
to see the strength of an army trapped inside.
Armed with her strength and wit, she prepares.

One soul centuries old. She stands alone.
She has defeated nations, nations have defeated her.
She has crawled on hands and knees for forgiveness,
to learn the true meaning of forsaken.

She has conquered Man, only to have Man try to lay claim to her.
All want to posses her. None know how to love her.
She has been to heaven, she has been to hell,
Now she stands alone, one soul centuries old.

Jessica H. Matarazzo-Hagel
Brooksville, FL

My Heart's in Your Hands

There's nothing I'd rather do
Than lay in your arms.
Those arms that are there,
There to catch me when I fall.
The arms connected to those hands,
The hands that hold my heart.
The heart that beats,
Beats for you and only you.
The heart that loves,
Loves your eyes and that smile.
That loves the sound of your voice,
And the smell of your body.
The heart whose love is given only to you
For always and forever,
'Cause you are my night, my day,
And my everything.
You are my other half,
The one that completes me,
And without being able to lay in those arms,
Those arms with those hands,
The hands that hold my heart,
Oh, that heart would break.

Nicole A. Trudden
Broad Channel, NY

The Fisherman

A day is born and darkness parts, he stares in fascination,
The sun awakes and stirs in hearts the day's anticipation.
The sea, so still and quiet, as if relaxed from sleep,
Is dressed now in a purple cape that's forty fathoms deep.
The sky takes on a wispy veil of pink and scarlet spears,
But soon will change to one of blue as the morning sun appears.
A gentle splash gives promise of a lively day ahead,
And breaks the magic silence of the sunrise overhead.
To hear the linen singing as it races from the reel,
A strike! The rod tip stiffens, and the angler's arms are steel.
The glass-like surface shatters in a flash of swirling white,
As the noble game breaks water, man or fish must lose the fight.
Far moved from all society, its haste and waste and din,
This is God's way of living, this is a fisherman.

Edward F. Pfister
Selbyville, DE

To a Good Man Who Will Never Be Forgotten

He was a great father
Who always knew best.
He did everything he could,
Never needed much rest.
He helped his family
Through thick and thin,
Taught them things
From deep within.
He was a mechanical wizard
From day one,
A foreman where he worked,
And I was proud I was his son.
We did things together,
And had so much fun.
I remember a lot of things,
Even back to age one.
So I love you, Dad,
I feel you're still with me.
Now you'll be in Heaven,
God bless your soul indeed.

Michael S. Swavely
Reading, PA

My name is Michael. I had a head trauma years back. I've come a long way since then. I'm better now than I was then. I'm smarter and an even better person now. I love to write poetry. I have a mother, sister, and brother. My father passed away of cancer on the fifth of January this year. The poem I wrote was written by me and read at the services. It was complimented by everyone I talked to. I loved my father very much and I miss him very much. I still think and talk about him.

Untitled

Tick-tock went the clock
Midnight ever nearing
Still no sound a-hearing
Ah, the telephone
Lifeline to my heart
And now a day spent alone

'Tis a game people play
And use the telephone
In many a strange way

The day has ended
Let it go and rest your mind
Learn to stand alone
Make no guesses
Give no yeses

On the morrow
Perhaps to mend your sorrow
Maybe yes
Maybe no
But for now
We do not know

Still not a sound
Nor a bell from that phone

Audrey Heranne-Mondress
Reading, PA

Ode to a Pesky Fruit Fly (An Elegy of Sorts)

He died, he died on the paper's obituary page.
How fitting, how unique, it might become the rage.

Think of it now; what could be more fitting
Than to go to "fruit fly Heaven" on that page sitting.

To have his mark left on that hallowed place
Was far from being a fruit fly disgrace.

One hard whack, one brutally crushing blow
And it was over, only a grease spot to show.

How better a way this earthly scene to leave
And to be wiped up carefully by my clean sleeve.

It's all over now, pesky fruit fly's gone to rest.
The way he left was probably the best.

Joseph K. Pinter
Beckley, WV

Heaven

Do the blind cry
Do the deaf listen
Do the lame yearn
Do the drunk hunger
Do the addicted linger
Do the lovelorn hope
Do the hopeless love

Only in dreams

George P. Schmidt
Fairview, NJ

My Friend

I like the nights with flashing stars,
The quiet streets without cars,
The tired lights of dark-some poles,
The lonely moon . . . I go . . . it goes with me.
Through all my life,
It saw my joy, my luck, my sadness,
My rainy days, my sunny days.
It knows my thoughts, my pains, my feelings.
It is my confidant, my friend.
My real friend in all its meaning,
I couldn't find on this land!

Nadia Naldonado
Monroe, NJ

First Love

Your heart beat and feelings for that special person.
It's the perfect reason.
Shouldn't let that one get away
so you wouldn't go astray.
Keeping together no matter what happens
in any situation.
Having trust and faith to depend
on each other's communication.
Making worthwhile commitments
and no resentments.
Love is the connection
best way to perfection.
First time is difficult for all.
But have someone to catch you
when you fall.
Beauty is truly in the eyes of the beholder.
Also to have someone to lean on their shoulder.
Never to regret
but not to forget.
Finding the right one to be around
Will make you get off the ground.
Feelings are in the best dealings
from the heart is the sealings.
Always be in the mind.

Salvatore J. Fertitta
No. Port, FL

The *Discovery*

The *Discovery* gracefully ascended as an assured shuttle
So smooth, serene, bright, and bold.
The pilot's voice exuded celestial calm
As she told of the flight's unfold.

The *Discovery*'s special mission lasted fifteen full days.
It was amazement we felt right from the start.
A prayer for the crew's safe return to Earth
Was sent straight up to them from our hearts.

Through the walk in space, 6.2 million miles away,
The crew completed a dangerous and skillful task,
And on Earth we were relieved upon their safe return to the ship
While we were all confident the work would last.

During the *Discovery*'s welcomed flight back home,
My husband immediately exclaimed,
"This was an amazing event that happened today
In the present history of our great USA."

I knew at that moment what he felt in his heart
As he expressed in his own special way,
"Everyone's child should eventually know
About the brave *Discovery*'s historic flight
In the month of November of long ago."

Ann K. Van Dyke
Henrico, VA

I was born February 1, 1946 in Lancaster, Pennsylvania. Many of my family members are teachers, artists, and musicians. In the 1920s, my mother was the principal, basketball coach, and Latin teacher at Paradise High School in Pennsylvania. My mother instilled the love of the arts in her family. I graduated from the Shenandoah Conservatory of Music and I taught elementary music in many schools in Frederick County, Virginia area. At this time, I love to write music and poetry. My "*Discovery*" poem was written at the moment it was televised. I enjoy writing poetry about historical events.

On My Wedding Day

What have I done? What did I just do?
What on this Earth ever possessed me to say "I do"?

What was I thinking? I must have been out of my mind.
What a great power, this thing love to keep me so giddy and blind.

I swore never to fall in love and I swore never to marry.
Both these vows I have broken and yet my heart is more merry.

It's something about him that makes my heart soar,
For each time I see him, I just want to be with him more.

His eyes are dark brown and speak volumes to me.
His hugs are like fuel blasting my restless soul free.

My pride demanded of me just say no!
But my lonely heart cried out, please don't let him go.

For so long we were alone, but I like it that way.
I did what I wanted when I wanted, and no one but me had a say.

But today, that's all changed, my maiden days are done.
With those two words, "I do," we are now different, one.

My heart is in the air and yet my knees are on the floor.
I want to stand beside him, but my eyes are on the door.

I want to run away, I just want to flee.
I don't want wifely duties or any responsibilities.

Tracy L. Taylor
Arlington, VA

Our Flag

Mighty, and with majesty
That waving flag o'er this land it flies,
High above and rippling in the wind,
It's peace and freedom we realize.

Busy, and always in a hurry,
We people of this land,
Only stopping now and then to give a look
At that commanding symbol for which it stands.

And so proud each American can be
Remembering those who fought for this flag,
Defending others in far-off lands
Maybe seeing our flag destroyed or in rags.

Yes, our flag has seen hard times
Through war and civil destruction,
But still on that pole so high,
It cannot be destroyed in thought or action.

Let's look up and remember as she stands
Our flag represents what sometimes we seldom say,
This flag flies for us all,
So be proud you are part of the USA!

Shirley Sorensen Hinz
Ault, CO

Poetry has opened many doors for me. It began as a hobby, putting together simple rhyming verse, which can encourage a writer to write, or a reader to read and enjoy more poetry, and I'm finishing a chapbook of my favorite pieces of poetry. Much of my poetry has turned into music and it is enjoyable to hear your words put into a song. I also love other types of writing, such as nonfiction. I volunteer, accept speaking invitations, manage a family business, and enjoy being a grandmother. I make time to write poetry and find it very relaxing in this busy world we all live in today.

The Dream

The day has arrived
The dream survived
It did not die
Do you know why
When you have hope
With wrong, you can cope
The road was rough
Until it was enough
To pull people together
To decide whether
It was worth the price
To make the sacrifice
Steering this great nation
In a whole new direction
Differences were put aside
For unity, the people cried
Arise, give yourself a hand
We're closer to the promised land
With new meaning, we sing
From every mountainside
Let freedom ring.

Jean C. Payne
Smyrna, GA

Online

We don't need to have a computer
To get online with God.
If we are forgiven of our sins and have Jesus Christ's
Holy Spirit we are online with God; Satan can't trod.
This online service is paid up for life,
For Jesus Christ give His life to pay the price
So we might receive eternal life.
To stay online, just give Jesus Christ
Your heart and soul.
Then He will keep you online till you have
Reached your final goal,
Which I hope is eternal life.
Then you will forever be online with God,
His heavenly host, and Jesus Christ,
Having been brought online through Christ,
Now living in a new life.

Henry V. Woodall
Four Oaks, NC

Winter Beauty

Winter has its own beauty
But you must look beyond
Chilly winds, ice, and snow
Only winter can imprison a house
With hanging icicles in various sizes
Tree branches are covered with sparkling ice
Maybe a layer of new fallen snow rests there
Birds look like puff balls in feeders
Picnic table and chairs look displaced and lost
How bright the dark of night becomes
With the beauty and silence of falling snow
Look up, watch the shimmering snowflakes falling
Thousands floating to earth, no two alike
Morning brings breathtaking beauty
On the blanket of snow many animal tracks
Are visible crisscrossing my yard
Wow, what a busy place as I slept
In wonderment, I think to myself
Do all these critters visit my yard
By the cover of night on a daily basis?
Bundle up, venture outside, take a walk
Appreciate the beauty of winter

Anita L. Rogers
Royersford, PA

I love the changes each season brings here in Pennsylvania. Each season has its own unique beauty. You could spend days outdoors and miss so much of nature's beauty. Hopefully we can all learn to slow down and appreciate the beauty surrounding us each day. Take time to be outside. Go for a walk and enjoy all the sights and sounds of nature, especially when the seasons change. When it is snowing late at night, I stand in my yard in wonderment, absorbing the silence and beauty.

Red Roses Filled Her Room

My darling mother
celebrated music and love
to live a life to be alive
Men came to dance to kiss
embrace have fun and paid
Red roses filled the room

Her hair was long so Irish red
She was not thin
I would say fat
A perfect secret no one knew
not neighbors wives or friends
A business that she dearly loved
red roses filled her room

I could not do what she did well
I worked from nine to five
When I came home the light went on
She smiled and looked so beautiful
Red roses filled the room

Cancer called the light went out the music stopped
We prayed we talked we cried
I lost
Who am I to judge
After all it was her life
Red roses filled her grave!

Helga Gross
Amargosa Valley, NV

My name is Helga Gross and I was born in Stuttgart, Germany. I grew up with my wonderful and hardworking grandparents in a tiny village called Grunbach, or the Black Forest. Twenty years ago. my dream came true and I came to America. I was twelve years old when I read Goethe's poems of beauty and power, which inspired me to want to write as well. Today I live at Helgaland in Amarosa, Nevada, with my four dogs, a cat, and a horse. Currently I am writing as well as composing a musical. My personal spiritual thinking is "Alle Nichtigkeiten des Lebens und Schaffens zu durchschauen und doch weiter zu Arbeiten!"

On That Day

When I stand before my Master
On that great and fateful day
When all the books are opened
And there's nothing more to say.

When He views the life I've lived
And all the deeds I've done
May He see the heart so full of love
For my father and His Son.

Will I have a crown in waiting
That I may lay at His dear feet?
Will there be precious jewels that I have gathered
As I've walked these earthly streets?

As I look into His loving eyes
When we gather around His throne,
My heart will then have answers
When He says, "Child, welcome home."

Elsie K. Meads
Siler City, NC

I fell in love with Jesus over forty years ago when He united me with my heavenly Father. Since that time, from time to time, when I meditate on His goodness, the Holy Spirit fills my mind with thoughts in verse form. I simply write them down. I really do not feel I can take any credit for them as I do not believe, within myself, I could write a poem.

Delivered

A postal worker delivering the mail
felt sick and tired, he looked very pale.
He sat in his truck on his afternoon break
and yelled out loud,
"How much more can I take?"
The December daylight soon faded away.
Some bags of mail were from yesterday.
He started his truck and drove to the river.
He looked at the bags filled with mail,
"If I don't deliver, I'll go to jail."
He opened the bags with a cold, cold shiver
and delivered the mail into the river.

Credit card users didn't get their bills.
Finance fees rose as high as the hills.
Sweethearts waited so long in vain,
for "snail mail" from lovers that never came.
Grandparents wondered, as weeks went by,
no thanks for cash gifts, they wondered why.
Sports people waited for tickets to arrive,
then watched on TV what they couldn't go to live.
Party goers waited for New Year's invites,
and felt forgotten on New Year's night.
Sometimes I wonder, what if I
had won a huge prize, but I had to reply?

Jessie Louise Corbin
Redwood City, CA

Blue Mist

Whenever you look into the skies
Love's always blinding your eyes
Relax, it's a brilliant type of state
To be given this wonderful fate

Every day is a dream
That old magic and mist, supreme
Beauty as seen in the heart
These souls shall never be apart

Envy the colors of paradise
Knowing life is never the price
Eternal moments are always there
My wife's blue mist, this I adore and care.

Derick Josey
Leesburg, VA

The Glacier

Against a backdrop of glacial white
I pause a moment to stop and write

Absorbing sight, sound and pristine air
I spin around to turn and stare

Above ice flow's unearthly glow
The glacier's head snakes far below

Twisted pillars form crevasses deep
Pointed shards, jagged, steep

A thunderous boom echoes off ice-carved rock
Moving past to present on a millennial clock

Never ending, retreat, advance
I must give more than parting glance

Etched in my memory, crisp, cold, and bright
I'll not forget the glacial white.

Lori L. Robinson
Livermore, CA

Sunshine Bunch

Adam and Eve had it made, they had a perfect home,
But they goofed, they couldn't leave the forbidden fruit alone.
They had it easy, no worries or cares, and plenty to eat,
They didn't have house payments or any bills to meet.
It seems like only yesterday, we were in school having fun,
Now we're with the Geritol crowd, thinking of what we've done.
I wonder if Moses and Noah had arthritis in their day,
I would love to talk to them to hear what they would say.
And look how old Sarah was when she had that baby boy,
If that happened to us, we would not count it as joy.
Our Advil, aspirin, and Tylenol, we cannot leave alone.
We're not the only ones to have aches in every bone.
The decisions we face when we get out of bed,
Do we put our left shoe on first, or the right one instead?
Some of us are bothered by the cold, some can't stand the heat,
We have headaches, backaches, and bunions on our feet.
The young people laugh at us, the things we do and say,
They think that we know nothing, we're just old and gray.
Each gray hair and wrinkle, we have a story to tell,
We're proud to be senior citizens, that sums it up pretty well.
We may have funny habits, and say silly things and such,
But we're also full of love and concern, we're a happy bunch.
I'll share this little tidbit with you, if I'm not too bold.
On my next birthday coming soon, I'll be eighty years old.

Betty S. Hall
Roanoke, VA

353

Happy (Belated) Halloween

On Halloween eve, children wear masks
And costumes to welcome back the
Spirits of the dead. They go from
Door to door seeking tricks or treats,
Just to shed their masks and costumes
At the end of the evening to show who they are.
Happy (belated) Halloween,
Pumpkin pies (fertile crescent loaves).
The spirit of Halloween has arrived.
Happy Halloween. Remember the lord
Of darkness. Let the lord of darkness
Cross over into our world. Do you
Believe in ghosts, demons, witches,
Warlocks, fairies, nymphs, werewolves,
vampires, elves? Do you believe in
Giants? Let us all combine our
Might, and cast just one more evil
Spell tonight, and to all have a
Happy Halloween,
He, he, he, he, he.

Robert V. Hicks
West Chicago, IL

A Forest Gone Forevermore

Why did you cut down the trees?
A forest once swayed with the breeze.
The birds and animals lost their homes.
Looking for shelter, now they do roam.
God's beauty forever gone, a forest forlorn.
To look at the forest that once belonged,
A sight that breaks my heart, like a sad song.
Why did you cut down the trees?
Was it for money, just for greed?
Life here will never be the same.
As the forest is forever gone, a shame.
You're the one that we all do blame.
Why did you destroy Mother Nature at her best?
I thought you were better than the rest.
As money and greed took first place,
How can you show your face?
The forest is forever gone, no shelter from the storms.
Owls that hoot have found refuge in my trees, a new dorm.
Birds, rabbits, deer, raccoons, all these animals and many more
Moved to my trees in the backyard, since the forest is forever gone.
Why did you destroy the forest,
A safe haven for all God's creatures not around?
God is shedding tears as the rain is falling down upon the ground.
No more trees stand and sway with the breeze; what goes round
Truly comes around, as this forest is gone forevermore.
Greed and money will never win,
God will let the trees grow a forest once more.

Linda G. Hunt
Chesterfield, SC

355

Hard Times in 2010

I have to smile, for most of our
hard times, we make ourselves.
I was taught to count out what
you have before you got it.
Put a few cents aside for a rainy day.

We were hard workers and believed
in cookie jars; only time
something came out was with our own hand.
Of course, no interest there.

Of course we bought a home,
but we look how it was going to
pay its way,
and a car on house and slay.
Times have changed, I must say.

Jenie A. Clark
Searsmont, ME

God gave us love and hands to help others that have less, and through these hard times, we must reach out to all ages. I have seen good times and hard times, but don't do it alone. We are all teachers in life. I am eighty-six years old and I have two sons, five grandchildren, and nine great-grandchildren. I love to write, paint, camp, and send painted cards to shut-ins. You live for the day, plan for tomorrow, and keep your eyes open. This is a lesson to your heart for what we can do for others. You'll find it will come back double.

More Valuable Than Your Abuse

You don't know me
very well.
I'm of value,
can't you tell?

Far more valuable
than your abuse,
not a mere toy
for your use.

A sophisticated lady,
complex, intricate, cultivated taste.
Barbaric ways
will never get you to first base.

Gladys B. Nance
Gray Court, SC

This poem was written to say to mankind that I will never lower my standards to please others! Sometimes we lower our standards to those set by others of who they think we are, but ladies of high moral values should never settle for simply a handsome face in choosing their partners in life or for life. Nor should we settle for abuse to keep a person in our lives. We should never devalue ourselves to please others because we are far more valuable than their abuse. I am married to James Nance and we have a son named Nikki D'Angelo Nance.

In Search of Sleep

When in my bed I've tossed and turned,
There is a lesson I should have learned.
My nocturnal activity cannot be abated
While my wakefulness center is stimulated.
The sources of stimulation, if I know the facts,
Are the brain and the muscles, which I must relax.
Letting all of my muscles fall right through the bed
And thinking of nothing should calm down my head.
But then, I really don't know if this . . . works for me . . .
For even when trying, I can't stay awake . . . to see . . .

Robert L. Brown
Greenville, SC

systole

metered liquid moment
slow-fast
muscled forth gently
rhythm-rhythm
double-measured clambering code
yes-yes
relentlessly hammering outwards
in-out
fractured sequential flood
moment-moment
instant erosion rebirth

John C. Cromie
Albany, NY

The Passage

My body sits still with the sand.
My eyes invoke the patterns the waters flow,
Invigorating my spirit.
My body sits still.
With the sand, I stay grounded.
My place of peace has always amounted;
Separate from dissonance,
I keep it bounded.
The tender, heartful climate
Only let out when
My body sits still.
My mind is sigh-lent,
My eyes invoke the patterns.
Leveling out, collecting,
I have it.
After resetting, I dash; split.
Slowly, the feeling follows,
Overriding the hidden sorrows.

Hali S. Parsons
Los Angeles, CA

Lost Dreams . . . Where Did They Go?

Lost dreams are not forgotten ones,
They linger just beyond
The labyrinths of the mind and heart
In memories so fond.

We treasure them like jewels,
Placed so carefully away
Taken out to cherish on a rainy,
Cloud-filled day.

They keep the hope of all that's good
Within an easy grasp.
They're waiting, hiding just close by,
And might be our next task!

Barbara Notestine Moulder
Bedford, VA

Your Love Is Like Rain on a Field

Your love is like rain on a field,
Nourishing and much needed.
Your love is beautiful like a delicate flower,
Filled with vibrancy and uniqueness.
Your love is forever like a never-ending story;
It lasts till the end of time, is filled
With wise words and eternal hope.

Dorcas A. Petite
Waldorf, MD

Choice

Country is the heart we unfold.
Government is like a child to scold.
It is a vision in growth we want to hold.
Never should it be a single control.
Given in freedoms for all people to unfold.

We bear as citizens in time a note
This choice will make it a goal.
Everyone's life in all times must be whole.
Government needs tending to keep it in control.
People give it life by the choices they unfold.
If it is given in truth, it will then be something to behold.

Stan G. Coveleski
Statesville, NC

Foggy Illusions

Dawn was slowly coming
Through the thickness of the fog
It seemed mystical and forthcoming
As I looked across the bog

In a shroud of illusion
A lone heron is flying high
He sounds in my conclusion
Like a wolf pup in the sky

In a shroud of quiet and serenity
Romantic figures seem to dance before me
If this is what it's like in eternity
It would certainly mimic my place to be

My senses are being overtaken
In the heavy moisture-laden air
I'll revel in it before it is forsaken
By the brightness of day becoming fair

Linda A. Goltz
Redding, CA

Honeybee

Bonnie-Bonnie, my honey.
Like the axis, turns the world,
worth far more than money.
God's petite, precious pearl.

Busy, busy little bee
storing honey in her hive.
Illustrious queen to see
buzzing here and there, alive.

Be careful, don't ignite.
Drones, convoys are swarming.
Skirmish, great odds—fight.
Choos, dandle warming.

Bonnie, Bonnie—honeybee
makes life so worthwhile.
So full of energy, funny,
wearing a blissful smile.

Bonnie, Bonnie—honeybee,
coterie, they swiftly flee.

Alma Ann Williams
Vardaman, MS

I have a very dear friend that has helped me travel the stormy road after my husband died. One day, she said, "Write me a poem," so here it is, all about her and her family. God gave to me the joy of words, how to use them to paint pictures of people, to express happiness, sadness, and humor. "Bless the Lord, oh, my soul, and all that is within me, bless His holy name," Psalms 103:1.

Dream Love

A love that lives forever
Is what we seek to find
The good and bad together
The mountains we must climb
When darkness falls upon me
I keep the dream alive
Only then you come to see
I need you to survive
Each tingle from your finger
The moment that we touch
The shivers that still linger
I need your love so much
Our hearts are linked as one
Each beat in perfect time
A kiss before the sun
Makes me wish that you were mine

Sue A. Smoot
Grantsville, MD

God, You, and Me

See the flowers grass and trees
See the rivers lakes and seas
See the deer birds and bees
See the clouds sky and galaxy
See the people friends and family
All made by God for you and me

See the stripped-out land and burned-out trees
See the oil cans and other floating debris
See our wildlife condemned so carefree
See our lust greed and enemies
See the atomic age missiles and artillery
Our thanks to God from you and me.

Joseph Thomas Jr.
Wheeling, WV

After living seventy-six years in Brooke County, West Virginia along the beautiful Ohio River, thirty years working at Weirton Steel Company, eleven years as park manager and golf course superintendent at Brook Hills Recreational Park, I learned to like and appreciate the wonderful works of Mother Nature. I saw the pollution of the Ohio River from sandy beaches to muddy, oily bottom and banks. I fought in World War II and saw the tragedies of war. I've seen the friendly way of life interrupted by terrorism throughout the world. All of these things inspired me to write this poem.

Untitled

I had stolen downstairs to witness the last ruby red sapphires
Glow and fall silent in the hearth slowly they dimmed, gradually
fading away
But alas I said to myself why such a beauty and pleasure be stifled
Torn up tissue paper and scrunched up newspapers these forlorn and
tragic tools
Would be all that would rekindle my sweet fire
So it could once again flood the hearth with its warm glow
With the lighter in my hand I set to work to start anew
But the first try failed smoldering to ashes
The second, the third, fourth, and fifth
Moaning in despair my heart ached to save the little burning vision
of hope
Finally on the last attempt a flicker . . . a flame . . . a fire!
I rejoiced feeling happy and fulfilled a weight lifted off my shoulders
I lay and watched as a new mother watches her child
Simultaneously feeding nurturing it keeping it alive
And it was a child dancing on the ashes of old
It was life, it was new, it was hope that burned inside of me—hope
Late into the night my head drooped and my eyes shut and my body
slowed . . .
I awoke early in the morning laying by the hearth—back to reality
To hurt and anguish to sorrow and despair
Questions were thrown at my face all I could do was smile to myself
And say barely above a whisper—hope
For there is always hope for those who believe
Always a radiant light at the end of the tunnel
Always an unwavering flame in the endless darkness

Olivia O'Connor
Marshfield Hills, MA

My Buddy Nick And Me

My buddy Nick has Cerebral Palsy you see
His body is so tight but his mind is so free

His smile & laughter will light up the world
His eyes are telling me his disabilities are no more

He can think with his body & stay locked in this world
Or think with his mind & go out & explore

He thinks with his mind & teaches me
That if I look around I too can see

Look up, look down, just look all around
& you can create who you want to be

Life is a choice, your mind holds the key
Just open it up & you will see

Be this, be that, be anything
Your mind has endless possibilities
My buddy Nick said to me

Toni Gates
Heath, OH

Characterization

Without occurrence and wanting to occur perfect
Preference came roseal
Rooted
Blood-colored
Rich
A pulse of verge and symbol icon behavior
Unpolished and sure-footed
Solidarity invited a subtenant and wanting to be
Beneath too movement went beyond
Substantive with stem and more deep rooted
A step-down compared to a step-up
The purpose doesn't develop much without cause
Raising reason and giving rise separate and set apart
From redeft regent
Variegated a red rose to black
A welcome to contrast
A tenderfoot and temperance

Camille Snowden
Fairfield, CA

Index of Poets

9 781608 800407